Fire Up Your
POWER
TOOLS

A Practical Handbook for Using the Gift of Tongues

LINDA MARKOWITZ

Fire Up Your Power Tools

© Linda Markowitz 2018

2nd Edition 2019

Cover Photo: Michael Cairns – wetorangestudio.com

Dictionary References are taken from http://www.webster-dictionary.org

ISBN: 978-1-731357-91-5

Publisher: Linda Markowitz Ministries

PO Box 1899 ~ Apopka, FL 32704 ~ LindaMarkowitz.com

DEDICATION

I respectfully dedicate this book to my friend, Brenda Wallace.

Your faithful obedience to loan me two well-worn

cassette tapes changed my life forever.

May your reward be incalculable.

A SPECIAL THANK YOU

My heartfelt gratitude to Thelma Campbell

whose fervent intercession in tongues

awakened my heart to the power of

interpreting the language of the Holy Spirit.

TABLE OF CONTENTS

CHAPTER 1

GOD'S GRACE IS SUFFICIENT FOR ME

I invite you to join me on my journey which began when I was five years old. My young years were filled with chaos, sadness and confusion. My mother died shortly before my sixth birthday, and my father was an over-the-road truck driver who was gone more than he was home. About a week after our mother was buried my father had to go back to work and left me and my younger sister and infant brother in the care of an alcoholic aunt. She and my uncle, who was also an over-the-road truck driver, had two children. Because I was the oldest, by default, I became the adult in a household with five children — myself, my sister and brother, my two first cousins, and a dysfunctional aunt who was falling down drunk every day before noon. That experience caused me to grow up really fast and taught me responsibility at a very early age.

Thankfully, at least once a week, my aunt would go to the grocery store first thing in the morning. Therefore there was food in the house, but I quickly came to know that, if we were going to eat any time after noon, I would have to find us something to eat. In essence, I became the mother of four —actually five, including my aunt—and I developed survivor mentality at the age of six.

My mother had been a Catholic and my father wanted to keep my sister and me somewhat involved in the Catholic church, but because he was gone most of the time, he had to leave the responsibility of getting us to church in the hands of his siblings. Consequently, we weren't in church very often. I did have my First Communion but have very little memory of my Catholic roots beyond that.

When my father was home between road trips, he would sometimes take us to visit his parents. Those were very special times for me and the only days during those years that I remember having the luxury of being a child. My paternal grandmother was a doting, loving woman who was a devout Baptist. If we were visiting on a weekend, she would insist that all of us dress up and go with her to the old country church that she belonged to. I vividly remember the sweltering hot church she so faithfully attended. I loved my grandmother and particularly liked sitting close to her in church because she always had a fan. The only relief I could get from the heat would be when I could catch a breeze as she fanned herself. I remember having to sit perfectly still on hot wooden pews because she made it clear that it was dishonoring to Jesus to squirm in His house. I particularly remember how difficult it was to sit still during the singing. There was just a creaky upright piano and a few voices leading the small congregation in a few old Southern Gospel favorites. I loved those happy songs. They etched something in my heart.

My grandmother loved the Lord and talked to Him and about Him as if He was a member of the family. She is the one who began to tell me about Jesus. She instilled a curiosity in me about her special friend, who I knew lived in her house, but I never saw.

When I was nearly eight years old, my father took us to Nashville, Tennessee to live with a woman who had been a friend of my mother. Her husband worked an over-the-road trucking job with my father, so we were once again in a household without a man present most of the time; but, this time things were different. This wonderful woman had two children that I loved, and she was a great mother. She took my brother, sister and me into her family as if we were her own children and, for a brief time, I was no longer the oldest in the household; and, I had a mother. Her children became like a sister and brother to me and I was very happy being a part of a loving family.

I was so contented during those days. My newfound 'Mom,' who I called Mama Maureen, loved the Lord and also happened to be another devout Baptist who took all five of us children to church regularly. At home she played the piano. We would gather around her old upright piano and she would teach us to sing old Southern Gospel songs. I remembered some of those songs from having heard them at my grandmother's church and something awakened in me. Under Mama Maureen's care, what my grandmother had imparted to me began to stir again. I desired to know the Jesus they knew.

Unfortunately, the time we stayed in Nashville was short-lived. We soon relocated to Indiana and for a while lived with a family we were not related to. My father then remarried and we remained in Indiana.

My beloved Mama Maureen died about two years later. My grandmother also died when I was ten years old. The spiritual embers that had been lit by my grandmother and sparked by Mama Maureen seemed to die along with them. It was decades later before I met Jesus for myself.

CHAPTER 2

RIP-ROARING START!

Flash forward quite a few years later. I was now a young, divorced mother of two daughters. My girls attended school at the local Assembly of God church, and the school was hosting a fundraising concert featuring a guest musical ministry team known as the Happy Goodman Family. Both of my daughters had been active in selling tickets for the concert and I had bought most of them. The school highly promoted the event and my girls wanted me to take them to hear the special singing. Initially, I wasn't at all interested and planned to just drop them off for the night and enjoy some "me time." That plan changed when I heard that the Goodman family sang Southern Gospel music. My memory went back to those wonderful times at my grandmother's church and around the piano at my Mama Maureen's house singing those songs. I decided to go to the concert. My daughters and some of my friends had a 'girls' night out' and went to the church to hear the Happy Goodman Family sing.

It began as a cheerful evening. The Goodmans sang some of those happy songs I remembered but, toward the end of the concert, the music changed from bright and peppy to something much more moving. I became aware of something faintly familiar stirring in my heart and it accelerated quickly. I can best describe it as a race car driver revving up his engine before the start of a race. It seemed as if I was preparing to enter a race. In the last few minutes of the concert the lead singer, Vestal Goodman, delivered a salvation message and gave an altar call. By what I now know to be the power of the Holy Spirit, I was drawn to respond to that call. I let my foot off the brake and walked out of my seat. I was sitting near the back of the church and don't remember making that walk. It seemed that I was at the front of the church as soon as my feet hit the aisle.

I found myself standing in a prayer line with about 15 other people waiting my turn for Vestal to pray for me when I sensed a large and commanding, but very inviting presence come and stand in front of me. My eyes were closed, so I didn't see anything, but I had a deep knowing that I was not alone. As soon as I was aware of the presence, I bowed my head to acknowledge it and fell backwards into something I can only describe as a firm, comforting hug. There was no one standing behind me. I was later told that I fell flat on my back on the floor, but I have no remembrance of that and was not hurt at all. While on the floor, that same powerful presence which had stood in front of me now seemed to move over me. I don't remember that presence touching me, and I didn't see or hear anything, but I was very aware that an exchange was taking place.

Something was being removed from me and, in exchange, I was being given something that I readily accepted.

Vestal and the ushers assisting her were several people away from me when I fell. When Vestal did get to me, I was told that she didn't pray for me at all; she simply waved her hankie over me and said, "You got it, honey; you got it,' and moved on to the next person in line. I got something alright! I was gloriously saved.

For me, responding to Vestal's call by stepping out of my seat and going to the front of the church was my way of asking Jesus to take my life and change me. I don't remember saying those words but, in my heart, I was aware that I was fully consenting and yielding to Vestal's invitation.

Apparently, no one prayed for me to receive the baptism of the Holy Spirit. While I was on the floor, He just came over me and, at the same time, sprang up from a place that had been awakened deep inside me. I find it impossible to find the words to describe that moment. Somehow, I became keenly aware that the Holy Spirit was inviting me to allow Him to completely overtake my life. I don't remember verbally saying, 'yes,' but I do know that I fully consented in my heart and did not resist. My experience was much like those of Cornelius' household.

> While Peter yet spake these words, the Holy Ghost fell on all them which heard the word. And they of the circumcision which believed were astonished, as many as came with Peter, because that on the Gentiles also was poured out the gift of the Holy Ghost. For they heard them speak with tongues, and magnify God (Acts 10:44-46).

Within minutes of accepting Jesus as my personal Lord and Savior, I was lying on the floor and received the infilling of the Holy Spirit with the evidence of speaking in tongues. I have no recollection of having received any previous teaching on the baptism of the Holy Spirit and honestly do not remember ever having heard anything about Him. But, when I willingly acknowledged that presence and yielded to that 'hug,' I became awakened to the precious Holy Spirit of God. I was completely filled with His presence and received an immediate and flourishing spiritual language.

> Within minutes of accepting Jesus as my personal Lord and Savior, I received the infilling of the Holy Spirit with the evidence of speaking in tongues.

After what seemed to be a long time, someone helped me to my feet and took me to a nearby pew where I sat speaking in my new language for several minutes. My friends saw to it that my daughters and I got home. Over the next few days, about three days if I remember correctly, every time I opened my mouth to speak, I would speak in tongues. I could still speak in English; the Holy Spirit didn't hijack my ability to speak. I could freely use my native language; but every time I opened my mouth, my first words would be in tongues and I just yielded to that. Because I had two young daughters and needed to communicate with them, I did speak in English, but only as necessary. I remember constantly using my new language and talking with my girls, too, but there was no frivolous conversation in those first few days.

My salvation experience was remarkable. I was saved, baptized with the Holy Spirit, and received my gift of tongues all in one night.

Shortly after I was saved, Brenda Wallace, a woman I had met previously and knew to be a good Christian, loaned me two cassette tapes. One was a teaching by Kenneth Copeland on faith, and the other a teaching by Marilyn Hickey on praying in tongues. I now know that by using something as simple and ordinary as two cassette tapes, God, in His infinite grace, gave me great speed in the things of the Spirit when I was yet a babe in Him. I devoured those teachings. For no particular reason, the first teaching I listened to several times was by Kenneth Copeland. From that teaching I learned about faith and how vitally important it was to my relationship with the Lord.

Brother Copeland's words seared my heart and the message of faith has only grown in me since then. The principles in that teaching are still an anchor for my life today and I draw from their wealth daily.

I had never heard of Kenneth Copeland before listening to that cassette, but he spoke with such power and authority that I was fully persuaded what he said was true. I am deeply and eternally grateful to God for this obedient servant who spoke such profound truth to me. I did not doubt the word of faith message when I first heard it and believe it strongly to this day. Faith in Jesus Christ has become a beloved and constant companion in my life.

From the teaching by Marilyn Hickey, I learned that I could strengthen my inner being by praying in tongues. Marilyn said I could pray in tongues all the time, and that I could do it at my will. Since I was so new in Christ, even though I knew nothing about either Kenneth Copeland or Marilyn Hickey, I trusted Brenda who had given me those two teachings. I used my newly-found faith, believed every word Marilyn said and decided to put a plan in action to help my new gift of tongues grow.

Within a month of my salvation, using what I had learned from Marilyn Hickey's teaching, I began training myself to pray in tongues all the time that I wasn't eating or talking. I put little notes everywhere that asked the question, 'Are you praying in tongues, or simply AYP (Are You Praying)?' I had those notes all over my house, in my car, and at my office. I kept moving the notes around so they wouldn't become so familiar that I would ignore them. I wanted that message to catch my attention. Every time I saw one of those notes, I would start praying in tongues again. It took discipline, but I was highly motivated to use my new language and within a few short months, I developed the habit of praying in tongues without ceasing. Marilyn Hickey said I could, and that settled it for me. Sometimes the naivety of new-born believers is so refreshing and energizing. I was a fresh, clean slate and did just what Marilyn taught on that cassette.

Using faith in Jesus helped me incorporate into my everyday life what Kenneth Copeland and Marilyn Hickey had taught me. I received a very extensive prayer language the night I was saved and the more I exercised that gift, the more it expanded. The Holy Spirit was making Jesus very real to me. The more I prayed in tongues, the more my faith strengthened, and my new-found life in Christ was off to a rip-roaring start.

Many years later I had the opportunity to meet Marilyn Hickey and personally thank her for her obedience to teach the truth, and told her how powerfully God had used her in my life. I may have to wait until eternity to meet Kenneth Copeland face-to-face, but someday I will surely give him my deepest heartfelt thanks for his obedience to teach the uncompromised word of faith. I never hear the song, "Thank You for Giving to the Lord," without thinking of these two faithful people and the other powerful and selfless generals in the faith that God has placed in my life. All of them have imparted spiritual truths into my life, helping me mature in my walk with Him. Brenda with her two cassette tapes, Kenneth Copeland and Marilyn Hickey, are truly gifts from heaven to me. My heart sings with gratitude for each of them and for their obedience to help them much which had believed through grace (Acts 18:27b).

The more I prayed in tongues, the more my faith strengthened, and my new-found life in Christ was off to a rip-roaring start.

I am deeply and eternally grateful to Brenda Wallace who put those two cassette tapes in my hand. She was surely following the leading of the Holy Spirit. Her obedience and generosity in loaning me those two teachings, along with my insatiable desire to receive anything the Lord had for me, laid a firm foundation for my entire walk with God. It is explicitly clear to me now that my relationship with the Lord could have taken an entirely different path if it had not been for the obedience of one woman and two well-worn cassette tapes. Those two teachings were heavenly gold to me, and I truly honor my friend Brenda Wallace, and have the deepest respect for Kenneth Copeland and Marilyn Hickey.

CHAPTER 3

HEAVENLY GOLD

I immediately began attending the church where I was saved. After a few months, it became apparent that others weren't as excited about my gift of tongues as I was. Some well-meaning people from my church tried to convince me that I was way overboard and out of bounds in using my gift of tongues (today that makes my heart smile). Looking back, I will admit that I was probably more than a little bit obnoxious and annoying because I wanted everyone to have what I had. I was shocked to discover that those who had been in the church for decades had no interest in speaking in tongues and had little or no spiritual depth. In my innocence, I thought I could fix that and was constantly trying to get them to join me in my parade. I was sincere, but sincerely wrong.

I believe those church members were sincere and were trying to instruct me from the light they had but, though they had been saved for many years, they were still very immature and misinformed. Thankfully, their counsel came way too late to change my course. By the time those discussions took place, I was soaring in the Spirit, living in peace, receiving sweet and continual revelation of Jesus and guidance from heaven. A prophetic gift was beginning to develop in me; I was enabled to see things to come in the future and know things previously unknown to me. I was overflowing with joy every day of my life and could barely contain my exuberant expressions of my newfound grace. I had experienced none of that prior to my salvation. Because I had no other point of reference in my mind, my salvation and the gift of tongues were inseparable and solely responsible for my new-found liberty.

Thankfully, I was fully aware that I had received something unique and valuable. I cherished the promise of the Father and wasn't tempted to let others who had no apparent victory in their lives talk me out of continuing in what I knew to be true. To this day, decades later, I still pray in tongues most of the waking hours of my day and I have often been awakened in the night by praying in tongues in my sleep. I live my life keeping my heart and my tongues connected, continually anticipating insight, direction and revelation.

As glorious as my beginning in Christ was, unfortunately for me, I prayed in tongues daily for over twelve years before I had any natural understanding about what I was doing. I know from my life experience that it is possible to speak in tongues every day of your life and never fully understand or utilize the potential of this supernatural power entrusted to the believer by God. In God's timing and grace, the Holy Spirit began to teach me how to work with Him while praying in tongues. I believe many Christians are just like I was during those first twelve years; speaking in tongues, zealous to do so; and, totally clueless to the purpose and power of such an amazing gift.

I call the gift of tongues my *power tool*, thus the title of this book, *Fire Up Your Power Tools*. With this amazing tool I have learned how to daily live a Spirit-led life filled with His great joy, how to pray into the future, and so much more. I want to share with you what I've learned. I truly wish someone had put a teaching like this in my hands when I was first saved and baptized in the Holy Spirit. If I knew then what I know now, there is no way to tell where I would be in my walk with the Lord today. If envy were permissible, I would greatly envy those of you who are newly baptized in the Holy Spirit. If you apply what you learn on these pages, I know you will begin operating in your gift of tongues well equipped to *Fire Up Your Power Tools* efficiently. You will glean a keen sensitivity to the Holy Spirit and be far ahead of some of us 'old timers.' It is my desire that this book helps you quickly become very valuable in the administrative work of God's Kingdom.

> With this amazing power tool I have learned how to daily live a Spirit-led life filled with His great joy, how to pray into the future, and so much more.

If you are saved, have received the baptism of the Holy Spirit, and already pray in tongues, I believe the following pages are filled with valuable truths from the Holy Spirit that will equip you to work with Him and help you find and fulfill the will of the Father in your life.

It is my prayer that this book will become a tool to accelerate you in your pursuit of God's highest and best for your life. I trust that in the years ahead I will find worn-out copies of **Fire Up Your Power Tools** all over the world, completely marked up and ready for the trash, but still held dear because the truths on these pages have opened the eyes of your heart to the mysteries of heaven in ways you have never known before.

Enjoy the Journey!

CHAPTER 4

YOU SHALL RECEIVE POWER FROM ON HIGH

This book is designed to be a training manual and, in order for you to get the greatest benefit from it, I want to briefly discuss the baptism of the Holy Spirit and the gift of tongues. There are multitudes of biblically sound teachings available on this subject so it is not my intent to give an in-depth explanation. I do, however, believe that if this book is to become a valuable training tool for you, we need to cover a couple of the basics and have a mutual understanding concerning the gift of tongues before we can move forward.

When Jesus commissioned His disciples to wait in Jerusalem until they received the promise of the Father, He didn't say, "Go there if you feel like it," or, "Please try to fit this into your schedule." Jesus did not give His disciples a suggestion. He commanded them to go to Jerusalem and wait there until they received the promise of the Father which was the gift of the Holy Spirit:

But the Comforter, which is the Holy Ghost, whom the Father will send in my name, he shall teach you all things, and bring all things to your remembrance, whatsoever I have said unto you (John 14:26).

And, being assembled together with them, [He] commanded them that they should not depart from Jerusalem, but wait for the promise of the Father, which, saith he, ye have heard of me (Acts 1:4).

Jesus knew intimately well the importance of His disciples receiving this gift.

On the Day of Pentecost, every believer in the Upper Room received the equipping and empowering of the Holy Spirit and began speaking in languages they did not know or understand. It was God's plan then, and it is God's plan now, that the gift of tongues be received and utilized by all His children:

And they were all filled with the Holy Ghost, and began to speak with other tongues, as the Spirit gave them utterance (Acts 2:4).

Cretes and Arabians, we do hear them speak in our tongues the wonderful works of God (Acts 2:11).

For he that speaketh in an unknown tongue speaketh not unto men, but unto God: for no man understandeth him; howbeit in the spirit he speaketh mysteries (1 Corinthians 14:2).

Jesus said that speaking in tongues is a sign that will follow those who believe in Him. According to Mark 16:17, all believers are to receive the baptism of the Holy Spirit with the evidence of speaking in tongues and are to regularly utilize this divine gift.

> And these signs shall follow them that believe; In my name shall they cast out devils; they shall speak with new tongues (Mark 16:17).

I believe Jesus is speaking in Mark 16 about every believer throughout all the ages of time, not a select few. *Them that believe* makes it really clear to me that Jesus put believing in Him as the only qualifier on who could and should speak in tongues. If the gift of tongues were only for certain people, or for a specific time in history, I am confident Jesus would have said so; and, nowhere in the Bible is it recorded that He changed His mind. I am a literalist when it comes to Scripture, and am a firm believer that Jesus said what He meant and meant what He said. If you believe in Jesus Christ and have made Him the Lord of your life, you must believe that the Bible is pure, unadulterated truth. That would then require you to believe that speaking in tongues is a valid and viable spiritual gift and is available to you. You would then also expect to receive the gift of tongues, and believe that this gift serves a distinct, current and relevant purpose in your life.

> 'Them that believe' (Mark 16:17) makes it really clear to me that Jesus put believing in Him as the only qualifier on who could and should speak in tongues.

I want to be explicitly clear that your salvation is not dependent upon whether or not you speak in tongues. All believers receive the Holy Spirit at the time of their salvation. The Holy Spirit is given to all who obey God and believe upon His Son, Jesus, and accept Him as Lord of their lives.

> And we are his witnesses of these things; and so is also the Holy Ghost, whom God hath given to them that obey him (Acts 5:32).

You can be very saved and never receive the baptism of the Holy Spirit with the evidence of speaking in tongues. Multitudes of Christians live long and useful lives without the gift of tongues. If you have accepted Jesus as your Lord and Savior, you already have the Holy Spirit living inside you. When believers receive the baptism of the Holy Spirit, they are not receiving something new; they are simply giving full liberty to the power of Someone they have already received and who dwells in them (John 14:17). They are giving this Someone, the Holy Spirit, permission to work with and through them.

The Holy Spirit longs to strengthen and lead you into the abundant life Jesus died to give you. But He will not force any of that on you; the choice is one hundred per cent yours. You are not a robot, and God doesn't treat you like one. You can receive the power of the Holy Spirit or reject it.

CHAPTER 5

SUPERNATURAL LANGUAGE

To simplify things going forward, let's ask and answer a few basic questions.

What is the gift of tongues?

In simplest terms, tongues is a supernatural language freely available to every believer and is received by asking in faith. It is the initial evidence of an experience subsequent to salvation known as the Holy Spirit coming upon a believer:

> He said unto them, Have ye received the Holy Ghost since ye believed? And they said unto him, We have not so much as heard whether there be any Holy Ghost (Acts 19:2).

Speaking in tongues happens when you receive by faith the gift of the Holy Spirit. Your natural human voice is used by the Holy Spirit to connect your spirit with the Holy Father God and His only begotten Son, the Master of the Church, Christ Jesus.

Tongues is an audible manifestation of this baptism. Tongues is a supernatural gift that enables a person who has made Jesus Christ the Lord of his life to speak in a supernatural language as the Holy Spirit prays to the Father using a natural human voice.

Tongues is a means by which the Holy Spirit speaks through a believer using a language unknown to the one speaking.

Tongues is the vehicle by which the Holy Spirit connects your spirit with the Father and Son and empowers you to work with them to do their business in the earth.

When you pray in other tongues, your human spirit prays by the Holy Spirit who lives in you using your human voice. You do the talking as He gives the utterance. By this method, the Holy Spirit helps you pray perfect prayers according to the Word of God. Tongues is not something the Holy Spirit does apart from you. That would make Him responsible for your prayer life. The Holy Spirit was sent as a helper to assist you in *your* prayer life, not to take over your prayers. Tongues do not force their way out of your mouth; you always have control of your gift of tongues. The Holy Spirit will never coerce you to do or say anything. If you are going to speak in tongues, you must willingly choose to do so and yield yourself to speak in a language you do not know.

What purposes does the gift of tongues serve?

The gift of tongues is a connector between the things of heaven and the things of earth. Praying in tongues enables the believer to have spirit-to-Spirit communication with God and gives us access to what He sees and knows. The Holy Spirit gives believers a spiritual language so we can communicate with God untainted by our personal agendas, bias or human input. God is a Spirit: and they that worship him must worship him in spirit and in truth (John 4:24).

> The gift of tongues is a connector between the things of heaven and the things of earth.

Praying in tongues is a spiritual tool that enables you to learn how to define the voice of God speaking to you. Learning how to hear and follow the leading of the Holy Spirit is crucial in the life of every believer. Praying in tongues helps you discern God's voice speaking to you and generates a momentum toward Him and His will that is always successful and prosperous.

One of the most important and exciting purposes for the gift of tongues is that it helps you build your own faith.

But ye, beloved, building up yourselves on your most holy faith, praying in the Holy Ghost (Jude 20).

Praying in tongues is a building tool. It helps the believer increase and strengthen his faith. Just as money is the standard of exchange for all earthly things, faith is the standard of exchange for all heavenly things. Believers must have strong faith in God in order to experience the benefits of heaven on earth and live productive and successful lives. Without faith we cannot receive anything from God. Everything God gives us is released from His hand by grace and received into ours by faith:

Without faith it is impossible to please God.

But without faith it is impossible to please him: for he that cometh to God must believe that he is, and *that* he is a rewarder of them that diligently seek him (Hebrews 11:6). And we can never please Him in our flesh.

So then they that are in the flesh cannot please God (Romans 8:8).

Are you unsure or confused about God's plan for your life? Another thing that happens when you develop a lifestyle of praying in tongues is that you begin to see an image of God's will for your life develop on the inside of you. Finding and fulfilling God's will for you is essential to living a life of peace and joy. Praying in tongues makes way for the Holy Spirit to bring clarity and understanding about God's plans and purposes for your life. Employing your gift of tongues will give you spiritual vision and can cause you to see things as God sees them. As your faith is strengthened, you can expect to be awakened to a spiritual perception that connects with your human understanding. You will begin to clearly see from God's point of view and receive heavenly ideas and instruction.

But the path of the just is like the shining sun, that shines ever brighter unto the perfect day (Proverbs 4:18 NKJV).

We will never be fully persuaded that every tomorrow we face can have a bright outcome unless we have the faith to believe that we are on the right path. Praying in tongues reveals our

God-given path and strengthens our faith to stay on it. Without the Holy Spirit leading us day-by-day we are destined to take costly detours and fall into more than a few muddy ditches along the way. Praying in tongues keeps us open and sensitive to God's direction and to the Holy Spirit's leading.

If you need clarity in any area of your life, praying in tongues can remove the nonsense running around you and eliminate the mindless clutter running through your brain. Using your *power tools* to purposefully receive revelation gives you heavenly vision. The Holy Spirit utilizes the gift of tongues to direct us to pray in accordance with the will of God. God always answers requests that are made in alignment with His will.

> If you need clarity in any area of your life, praying in tongues can remove the nonsense running around you and eliminate the mindless clutter running through your brain.

And he that searcheth the hearts knoweth what is the mind of the Spirit, because he maketh intercession for the saints according to the will of God (Romans 8:27).

And this is the confidence that we have in him, that, if we ask any thing according to his will, he heareth us: 15 and if we know that he hear us, whatsoever we ask, we know that we have the petitions that we desired of him (1 John 5:14-15).

Once you receive a direction from God, even if it is just a small piece of the overall puzzle, and even if there are no immediate changes in the situation, His peace and joy will come and you will have an unshakable confidence that you're on the right path. Praying in tongues doesn't always allow you to see the end from the beginning. God works with faith, time and other people. Full clarity and instant answers are few and far between; but, if you meekly and respectfully yield to your gift of tongues, you can fully expect to receive lucid insight on what part you play in the process, and what to do next.

When you pray in tongues, who is speaking to whom?

> For he that speaketh in an unknown tongue speaketh not unto men, but unto God: for no man understandeth him; howbeit in the Spirit he speaketh mysteries (1 Corinthians 14:2).

When you pray in tongues, the Holy Spirit uses your natural voice to speak to God the Father and God the Son. When you pray in tongues, you yield your spirit to the Holy Spirit who uses your natural, physical speaking ability to facilitate a conversation between you and God. When you speak in tongues, the language may, or may not be known by someone somewhere in the world, but it is definitely known by God, and unknown to you. Speaking in tongues is 'spirit-to-Spirit' language. When you yield your spirit to the Holy Spirit you are very much a part of the conversation. When praying in tongues, your heavenly language, the Holy Spirit can give you understanding and equip and empower you to do heavenly business on the earth both for yourself and for others. Tongues is a vital *power tool* in making you a fruitful partner in Kingdom business.

I have found that praying in tongues is the best way to access the ministry of the Holy Spirit. He is the teacher of the church (John 14:26). When you pray in tongues you do not pray words 'which man's wisdom teaches'. The words you are praying are what the Holy Spirit teaches, comparing spiritual things with spiritual.

Which things also we speak, not in the words which man's wisdom teacheth, but which the Holy Ghost teacheth; comparing spiritual things with spiritual (1 Corinthians 2:13).

All of God's power is exemplified in His love and praying in tongues is the language of love. In very basic terms, praying in tongues enables you to work with the Holy Spirit to bring love to earth.

Understanding these few basics about the gift of tongues gives us a mutual and firm foundation to build upon as we move forward. Please confirm in your heart that you agree with all these foundational basics concerning the gift of tongues.

- Tongues is a gift given by Jesus to all who believe in Him. It is not a gift for a chosen few. It has been given by Jesus to the entire Body of Christ.

- Tongues is a gift received by faith.

- Tongues is the initial manifestation of the gift of God known as the baptism of the Holy Spirit.

- Tongues is a supernatural language that connects heaven to earth and gives the believer access to the heart and will of God.

- Tongues builds the faith of the believer.

- Tongues is the Holy Spirit using your natural voice to speak to God.

- Tongues helps the believer recognize and define the voice of God speaking to him personally.

CHAPTER 6

THE TOOL THAT PRIMES THE PUMP

The baptism of the Holy Spirit is an event subsequent to salvation in which the Holy Spirit who is already with you is activated in you to do His greater work in and through you. That greater work is to magnify Jesus. Jesus cannot get any bigger than He already is; however, it is the job of the Holy Spirit to magnify Jesus in you and in the world around you. Receiving the baptism of the Holy Spirit activates His power in your life to be a witness of the goodness of Jesus. I see tongues somewhat like the tool that primes that pump.

Immediately after His resurrection Jesus gave the Holy Spirit to His followers.

Then the same day at evening, being the first day of the week, when the doors were shut where the disciples were assembled for fear of the Jews, came Jesus and stood in the midst, and saith unto them, Peace be unto you. And when he had so said, he shewed unto them his hands and his side. Then were the disciples glad, when they saw the Lord. Then said Jesus to them again, Peace be unto you: as my Father hath sent me, even so send I you. And when he had said this, he breathed on them, and saith unto them, Receive ye the Holy Ghost (John 19:21-22).

This is exactly what happened to you when you were saved. You received the Holy Ghost. When the Holy Spirit came into the Upper Room after the ascension of the Lord, He did not come to convert anyone. Everyone there had already received Jesus as Lord of their lives and the indwelling presence of the Holy Ghost. The Holy Spirit came to empower the followers of Christ and give them provision. He provided them with the spiritual equipment and power they needed to do the work assigned to them in the days ahead. He does the same thing today.

But ye shall receive power, after that the Holy Ghost is come upon you: and ye shall be witnesses unto me both in Jerusalem, and in all Judæa, and in Samaria, and unto the uttermost part of the earth (Acts 1:8).

'For in Him dwells all the fullness of the Godhead bodily' (Colossians 2:9 (NKJV). Even though Jesus' life on earth had been prophesied by the prophets, and His birth and lordship announced by an angel, He did not step into His ministry and all that had been prepared for Him until the Holy Spirit came upon Him. The natural man Jesus had no supernatural power until He was anointed by the Holy Spirit. Every miracle Jesus performed was done through the empowering of the Holy

Spirit. He was intimately acquainted with the power of the Holy Spirit and knew how necessary it would be for His disciples to receive everything the Spirit had to give them. Jesus knew that His disciples would not be equipped to accomplish the commission He was giving them unless they were empowered by the Holy Spirit.

Jesus placed such a high priority on His followers receiving the Holy Spirit:

> And I will pray the Father, and he shall give you another Comforter, that he may abide with you for ever; even the Spirit of truth; whom the world cannot receive, because it seeth him not, neither knoweth him: but ye know him; for he dwelleth with you, and shall be in you (John 14:16-17).

> And, being assembled together with them, commanded them that they should not depart from Jerusalem, but wait for the promise of the Father, which, saith he, ye have heard of me (Acts 1:4).

This fact alone is more than enough reason to seek a working relationship with this precious member of the Godhead. Every believer in Jesus Christ has a mission to accomplish for His Kingdom. I know from personal experience, and the testimonies of others, that it is impossible to find and fulfill God's will without the assistance of the Holy Spirit. Only the Holy Spirit can reveal our assignment and empower us to carry it out. We need the same infilling Jesus had to equip us to do the work He calls us to do.

Every person present in the Upper Room was baptized with the Holy Spirit and equipped with a language unknown to them. The initial manifestation that came with the impartation of the Holy Spirit on the Day of Pentecost was that every person present began to speak in an unknown tongue:

> And there appeared unto them cloven tongues like as of fire, and it sat upon each of them. 4 And they were all filled with the Holy Ghost, and began to speak with other tongues, as the Spirit gave them utterance (Acts 2:3-4).

If the early Church believers needed the baptism of the Holy Spirit with the evidence of speaking in tongues before embarking on the work entrusted into their hands, why would we think that we can do anything without Him and ignore the gift of tongues today?

> The initial manifestation that came with the impartation of the Holy Spirit on the Day of Pentecost was that every person present began to speak in an unknown tongue.

In my personal walk with the Lord there came a time when I became keenly aware that I have a specific part in the will of God to fulfill in my lifetime. I quickly came to recognize that I can do nothing for God. I can only work with Him to accomplish what He wants done in the earth. For me, learning how to work with God came through an understanding of how to yield to the Holy Spirit using my gift of tongues. My baptism in the Holy Spirit was NOT a means

38

for me to get more of Him. I received the Holy Spirit at salvation, just like you did. The baptism simply allowed the Holy Spirit to get more of me. It was only as I learned how to hear, surrender to and follow the leading of Holy Spirit that He could quicken and equip me to work with Him in the earth.

My goal is to help you understand the true benefits of speaking in our spirit language and the weighty significance of this precious tool given to us by God.

- Praying in tongues is a gift available to every believer in Jesus Christ and is a creative prayer tool.

  And these signs shall follow them that believe; In my name shall they cast out devils; they shall speak with new tongues (Mark 16:17).

- Speaking in tongues is a spiritual language that empowers the believer in Jesus Christ to communicate with God and equips him to live in the Spirit, walk in the Spirit, and know how to be led by the Holy Spirit of God.

  For as many as are led by the Spirit of God, they are the sons of God (Romans 8:14).

- Praying in tongues helps us develop in the fruit of the Spirit.

  But the fruit of the Spirit is love, joy, peace, longsuffering, gentleness, goodness, faith, meekness, temperance: against such there is no law. And they that are Christ's have crucified the flesh with the affections and lusts. If we live in the Spirit, let us also walk in the Spirit (Galatians 5:22-25).

- It also prepares us to be vessels through which the gifts of the Holy Spirit can manifest.

> But the manifestation of the Spirit is given to every man to profit withal. For to one is given by the Spirit the word of wisdom; to another the word of knowledge by the same Spirit; to another faith by the same Spirit; to another the gifts of healing by the same Spirit; to another the working of miracles; to another prophecy; to another discerning of spirits; to another divers kinds of tongues; to another the interpretation of tongues: but all these worketh that one and the selfsame Spirit, dividing to every man severally as he will (1 Corinthians 12:7-11).

Though many pray in tongues, the value of the gift is often missed. When believers pray in tongues, the Holy Spirit prays through us bypassing our intellect, mindsets, personal agendas and emotions. He covers all of our inadequacies and prays the perfect will of God.

> Likewise the Spirit also helpeth our infirmities: for we know not what we should pray for as we ought: but the Spirit itself maketh intercession for us with groanings which cannot be uttered (Romans 8:26).

Praying in tongues grants us a means by which we can pray the perfect will of the Father and be empowered to speak His truth and wisdom into our situations. Praying in tongues gives us access to the mind of God. It allows us to see through His eyes and grants us the ability to move out beyond time and space. Speaking in tongues uncovers hidden things and gives us clarity in obscured situations, and SO much more. Oh, what a holy gift!!! I believe that learning how to work with the Holy Spirit by employing the gift of tongues in our everyday lives is a vital necessity.

> For if I pray in a tongue, my spirit prays, but my understanding is unfruitful (1 Corinthians 14:14 NKJV).

In this verse Paul makes it very clear it is your spirit that prays in tongues. Your spirit prays using your natural voice. When believers pray in tongues, the Holy Spirit bypasses our natural mind and uses our natural vocal cords to give our spirit a voice. Praying in tongues is supernatural and will never be explained by natural reasoning so I encourage you to avoid the temptation to 'make sense' of this gift. Working through logic and human reasoning is a worn-out trap the enemy employs every time a believer begins to move toward anything supernatural. We receive the baptism of the Holy Spirit and the gift of tongues by faith.

> When believers pray in tongues, the Holy Spirit bypasses our natural mind and uses our vocal cords to give our spirit a voice.

> This only would I learn of you, Received ye the Spirit by the works of the law, or by the hearing of faith? ... that the blessing of Abraham might come on the Gentiles through Jesus Christ; that we might receive the promise of the Spirit through faith (Galatians 3:2,14).

I encourage you to use your faith concerning the gift of tongues; simply agree that God's ways are higher than yours, and leave it at that. Make a choice to cultivate and expand your tongues by faith in Jesus.

Because your spirit does the praying, you can do a number of other things and still pray in your heavenly language. I pray in tongues all day long and can function normally in all my regular activities except eating and talking, and so can you. The Holy Spirit doesn't pray through your brain; He prays through your spirit. Your natural brain is only involved in the process when an interpretation is necessary. I can pray in tongues all throughout my normal work day and still have total, acute mental focus on the natural things I'm doing. I am praying in tongues as I write this book.

CHAPTER 7

A LIMITLESS RESOURCE

'I thank my God I speak with tongues more than you all.' – *Paul, the Apostle of Christ (1 Corinthians 14:18 NKJV)*

My personal walk with the Lord has proven to me that it is not merely difficult, but impossible, to develop and maintain a vibrant, revelatory and uncompromised relationship with God without the baptism of the Holy Spirit and the gift of tongues. I am now fully persuaded that, in order for me to live a fruitful life and be an active co-laborer in the administrative business of God's Kingdom on earth, I must be empowered by the Holy Spirit and that my heavenly prayer language is fundamental equipment.

Praying in tongues and purposefully working with the Holy Spirit is a vital part of a healthy and victorious Christian life. I live my daily life intentionally interacting and engaging with the Holy Spirit, and the primary way I do that is by praying in tongues. I know that receiving the gift of tongues is necessary, and being well-trained in how to use that gift effectively is imperative. It is my heart's desire that this book become an important training tool to help you mature in using your gift of tongues.

> And these signs will follow those who believe: In My name they will cast out demons; they will speak with new tongues (Mark 16:17).

According to Jesus ALL believers should speak in tongues. The gift of tongues is for every believer and is every bit as supernatural as casting out devils and raising the dead; but some believers reject the gift of tongues entirely, and others who have received this precious gift have no grasp of its far-reaching extent or limitless capabilities. Unfortunately, then, for many believers, the gift of tongues remains a buried treasure and, when it is used, is rarely given the opportunity to develop to its highest potential. I pray this book changes that scenario in the lives of believers all over the world.

Jesus taught us to ask the Father for the power of His Kingdom in heaven to come to earth:

> Thy kingdom come. Thy will be done in earth, as it is in heaven (Matthew 6:10).

> And he said unto them, When ye pray, say, Our Father which art in heaven, Hallowed be thy name. Thy kingdom come. Thy will be done, as in heaven, so in earth (Luke 11:2).

He also taught us that it is the will of His Father for everyone who believes in Him to live an abundant life:

The thief cometh not, but for to steal, and to kill, and to destroy: I am come that they might have life, and that they might have it more abundantly (John 10:10).

An abundant life is a life filled with tangible expressions of the Father's goodness. It is a life filled with visible demonstrations of the love, wisdom, strength, peace, joy, provision and the power of God. Sadly, few Christians can say they are living the abundant life. The gift of tongues is a limitless resource of heaven to bring God's Kingdom to earth. It is a *power tool* given by God to help believers understand His purposes and equip us to live satisfying lives. I believe Spirit-filled Christians must learn how to use this dynamic tool and how to use it properly. My goal is to help you do that.

> The gift of tongues is a limitless resource of Heaven to bring God's Kingdom to earth.

I desire to stir the reader who has already received the gift of tongues to seriously contemplate and discover the multiple uses and benefits of this amazing gift. Believers don't work for God; we work with Him, *'for we are laborers together with God'* (1 Corinthians 3:9). The way we do that is through the empowerment of the Holy Spirit and learning how to cooperate with Him.

Now concerning spiritual gifts, brethren, I would not have you ignorant (1 Corinthians 12:1).

Prior to His crucifixion, Jesus spent considerable time instructing and preparing His disciples for the upcoming events. Jesus told them that He was leaving but was not abandoning them or leaving them comfortless, and that He would pray to the Father and the Father would send them another Comforter.

And I will pray the Father, and he shall give you another Comforter, that he may abide with you for ever; (John 14:16).

Jesus meticulously detailed the works of this Comforter and made it very clear that the Holy Spirit was Himself in another form and would never leave or forsake them. Jesus promised that the Holy Spirit would lead them into all truth.

I find it puzzling that teachings on the baptism of the Holy Spirit and the gift of tongues are so controversial and often radically divide the Body of Christ. Many Christians get very nervous and uncomfortable talking about the gifts of the Holy Spirit, and often, the subject of tongues holds the number one position on that list.

A study of the early church shows that after Pentecost there was no confusion about anything the Holy Spirit released to the believers, and controversy about the empowerment of the Holy Spirit was non-existent. On the contrary, it is apparent in the New Testament that the early believers fully accepted all of the workings of the Holy Spirit, including speaking in tongues, as a vital necessity and were eager and diligent to work with Him. They believed without question that His gifts were available to all who believed in Jesus Christ as Lord. Every leader in the New Testament was filled with the Holy Spirit, including Jesus:

And Jesus, when he was baptized, went up straightway out of the water: and, lo, the heavens were opened unto him, and he saw the Spirit of God descending like a dove, and lighting upon him (Matthew 3:16).

And the Holy Ghost descended in a bodily shape like a dove upon him, and a voice came from heaven, which said, Thou art my beloved Son; in thee I am well pleased (Luke 3:22).

And John bare record, saying, I saw the Spirit descending from heaven like a dove, and it abode upon him (John 1:32).

How far removed we are today from what the members of the first Church embraced so freely.

The subject of tongues raises a multitude of questions in itself but I have found that asking Spirit-filled believers what they are doing with the gift raises even more. Many in the Body of Christ have received the infilling of the Holy Spirit with the evidence of speaking in tongues but are completely unfamiliar with the myriad of purposes for this life-changing gift. The Holy Spirit has no limits other than what we put on Him by our neglect or unbelief. I want to break through any limits I have put on the Holy Spirit in my own life and I believe you want to do the same.

In my own personal and entirely unofficial survey I discovered that not one person I asked could articulately tell me what they were doing while praying in tongues. There were a lot of vague ideas and some pretty interesting guesses, but I did not receive one biblically clear answer. Spirit-filled Christians need to know the limitless potential behind yielding their gift of speech to the Holy Spirit.

My *power tools* have become the single most effective key to opening the doors of the supernatural and unlocking the power of God in my life. They reveal the resurrection power of Christ to me in ways that nothing else can. The gift of tongues opens my heart and eyes to the spiritual realm, allows me to see beyond natural circumstances, and gives me revelation after revelation of Jesus. My *power tools* sometimes escort me into a realm beyond myself and SO much more. I have experienced that praying in my spiritual language while listening to another minister gives me insight into the Word they share beyond what they might say. Praying in tongues while I read Scripture opens the Word of God to me in ways that nothing else can.

> My power tools have become the single most effective key to opening the doors of the supernatural and unlocking the power of God in my life.

I have learned that when I pray in tongues I operate more freely in the other gifts of the Holy Spirit as well. Often when I receive words of wisdom or discernment in a situation, I become aware that I have simply received an interpretation of something I had prayed earlier in tongues. I believe that happens because my human spirit is more open and submitted to the Holy Spirit when I pray in tongues and I constantly live in a state of readiness to work with Him. My desire is to work with my Divine Helper.

Are you a believer that has received the infilling of the Holy Spirit with the evidence of speaking in tongues yet, primarily because you don't know what else to do, rarely use the gift? When some believers pray in tongues they simply put their prayer language on cruise control and let it run amuck. You can speak in tongues and completely bypass the importance of what you are doing, but that is far from being the highest and best use of this valuable gift. Can God use prayers like that? Yes, of course He can, but there is a better use of tongues.

If you are a Spirit-filled believer who seldom uses your gift of tongues, or perhaps use it indiscriminately, never giving a second thought to its purpose or power, I trust that what you learn here will help you get past these very elementary uses of your personal spirit language. You may not have a clear concept of what praying in tongues accomplishes, but if you are open to receive revelation from the Holy Spirit, I believe He will use me to give you concise instruction on how to begin working 'with' Him in the administrative work of the Kingdom of God.

Even if you have been saved and filled with the Holy Spirit for years, I encourage you to look at Him with new eyes and make a new way for Him in your heart. I encourage you to embrace the mindset that praying in tongues is not something believers have to do when a pastor or church leader requests it, but that praying in tongues is something we get to do and should be doing regularly. What a tremendous privilege we have been granted by God to speak to Him in a heavenly language that only He knows. Through our communion with God in tongues, we co-labor with the Holy Spirit to utilize our most holy faith to bring the manifested presence of God and the limitless provisions of heaven to earth. It is nearly impossible to wrap our brains around that but, by faith, we can receive and operate in every bit of it.

If you want to grow in your working relationship with the Spirit of Truth, I am confident this book will help you. I invite you to read the following pages carefully and set your faith to benefit from what has taken me over 30 years to learn. I desire that this book becomes a practical working guide to assist Christians who have already experienced the baptism of the Holy Spirit and do speak in tongues, but perhaps have little or no comprehension of what is taking place when praying in their spiritual language. If that describes you, trustfully, the teaching on these pages will change that and will dramatically enhance your partnership with the Holy Spirit. As you read the following pages I trust you will find a very straightforward and uncomplicated view of the gift of tongues from the perspective of learning what you are doing while utilizing this inexhaustible resource from God.

Once you understand the limitless power behind your *power tools*, they won't be so neglected. The gift of tongues is a heavenly support system freely given to all believers. Refuse to despise, disregard, or ignore it. Your *power tools* give you a door of entrance into the realm of the Spirit, and you will love what is revealed to you there. Lavishly glean from what you learn here and I believe you will enter into a new and exciting working relationship with the Holy Spirit. If you open your heart to receive, what you learn on the pages of this book will change your relationship with the Spirit of Truth and Grace forever.

CHAPTER 8

THE EVERYDAY TONGUE

Would you like to have a personal audience with God without any outside distractions? People all over the world want to talk to their god. Paul the apostle tells us that we have a direct, uninterrupted connection to the One and Almighty Jehovah God when we pray in tongues. Tongues is the Christian's hotline to the only true God.

> For he that speaketh in an unknown tongue speaketh not unto men, but unto God: for no man understandeth him; howbeit in the spirit he speaketh mysteries (1 Corinthians 14:2).

Praying in tongues gives us a personal audience with God. When we get an audience with Him, we can expect supernatural intervention to follow.

Paul identifies two different manifestations and two different purposes for the gift of tongues. The Holy Spirit does not force Himself on anyone at any time and believers must willingly choose to work with Him in both of these manifestations.

One purpose for tongues is the ministry of the Holy Spirit to the Body of Christ in a corporate setting:

> And there are diversities of operations, but it is the same God which worketh all in all. But the manifestation of the Spirit is given to every man to profit withal. For to one is given by the Spirit the word of wisdom; to another the word of knowledge by the same Spirit; to another faith by the same Spirit; to another the gifts of healing by the same Spirit; to another the working of miracles; to another prophecy; to another discerning of spirits; to another divers kinds of tongues; to another the interpretation of tongues: but all these worketh that one and the selfsame Spirit, dividing to every man severally as he will (1 Corinthians 12:6-11).

This manifestation of the gift of tongues is given only at the will and leading of the Holy Spirit and is given to profit the entire assembly, not an individual person.

The second purpose of tongues is to empower and equip the individual believer and cause him to grow personally in his relationship with Jesus and authorize him to administrate Kingdom business. Out of that internal growth Jesus becomes magnified in us and we can then glorify Him in other areas. This second manifestation of tongues is what Paul refers to when he says, '*I would that ye all spake with tongues...*' (1 Corinthians 14:5a).

In this book we are only addressing the second manifestation of the gift of tongues; the personal equipping, empowering, and growth of the believer to glorify Jesus. I want to approach this expression from two dimensions. I am confident that there are more than two, but want to share with you the two that are life-giving to me. First, we will look at what I call my 'everyday tongue' and second, we will explore how to use our *power tools* to co-labor with the Holy Spirit to administrate the work of God's Kingdom in the earth.

I believe this book will not only educate you, but has come to you with the anointing of Christ to empower you to use your gift of tongues as precise tools for the purpose of helping you cooperate with the Holy Spirit in a greater way. I believe what you will learn here will enable the will of our good and generous Father God to come to pass in your daily life, in your family, and in your entire sphere of influence. I encourage you to take this last sentence as a personal word of encouragement straight from the heart of God to you.

No believer desires to be guilty of being ignorant in the things of God, and I encourage you to study to show yourself approved concerning the subject of how to co-labor with God in tongues. How you perceive the gift of tongues is crucial to expanding your ability to use this gift at its highest potential. Perception becomes your compass in life and, what you perceive becomes your reality, even if your perception is wrong. I want you to have a clear biblical perception of the gift of tongues. You have an amazing support system in your *power tools* that will help you gain God's best for His purposes, and I encourage you to use that support.

Once a believer in Jesus Christ is baptized in the Holy Spirit and receives the gift of tongues, he has the ability to pray in tongues any time, at will. The believer has total control over this

> All other gifts of the Holy Spirit come as He wills, but believers can access this form of tongues, this wonderful power tool of the Spirit, every day at will.

particular gift and is only limited by his own desire for the things of God and his willingness to yield to the Holy Spirit. I am sure there are countless ways to connect with the Holy Spirit but, in my personal experience, praying in tongues is the one that consistently supersedes all others in speed and efficiency. All other gifts of the Holy Spirit come as He wills, but believers can access this form of tongues, this wonderful *power tool* of the Spirit, every day at will.

In this chapter, we are going to take a look at what I believe is the most common way we can use our gift of tongues to co-labor with the Holy Spirit. This is a form of communing with God that I call my 'everyday tongue.' The gift of tongues is invaluable to me and my 'everyday tongue' is one that I make a conscious, purposeful choice to use, and I use it regularly. I believe every Christian should purposefully use their *power tools* and, by faith, intentionally co-labor with the Limitless One every day of their lives.

We receive supernatural reinforcement and support from heaven when we yield our natural speech to the supernatural gift of tongues. I can pray in my 'everyday tongues' as I go about my normal activities. All day I consciously yield to the Holy Spirit and, by faith, I receive everything I need that the Holy Spirit releases to my soul and body. What a deal!!! Praying in our 'everyday tongues' can be nearly effortless on our part and yet the results are life-giving and sustainable. Trust me, it can't get any better than that.

Throughout First Corinthians we see Paul attempting to convince the believers in Corinth to unite their minds and their spirits with the Holy Spirit of God. Paul wanted the Corinthians to learn how to connect with and release the God-given knowledge resident in their spirit and allow it to overtake their natural thinking. He wanted them, and wants us, to be built up in Christ and live holy, perfected and fruitful lives. One of the primary ways Paul instructed them to do that was by praying in tongues.

It is as normal for you to speak in your personal devotional heavenly prayer language as it is to breathe. You can pray in tongues anytime, anywhere. Paul says that he wished all believers would speak in tongues.

> I would that ye all spake with tongues, but rather that ye prophesied: for greater is he that prophesieth than he that speaketh with tongues, except he interpret, that the church may receive edifying (1 Corinthians 14:5).

Please note, Paul says that he wished all believers 'would' speak in tongues, not 'could' speak in tongues. Paul's other writings confirm he believed the gift of tongues was given to all believers in Jesus Christ. I can't emphasize enough that the gift of tongues is available for every Christian, everywhere, with no exceptions.

'*He who speaks in a tongue edifies himself, but he who prophesies edifies the church*' (1 Corinthians 14:4 NKJV). In the context of this passage, edification is self-intercession. It means to pray in a manner that strengthens and builds up the one who is praying. After several years of praying in tongues daily someone asked me how much time I spent praying for myself. I had to answer honestly that I rarely prayed for myself. Initially that answer puzzled both me and the one who asked the question. This particular person was in the middle of a severe trial and had been praying for herself in her native language for several hours a day for weeks, but the situation was not improving. In comparison to this woman's life, mine was peaceful and victorious and she thought perhaps she wasn't praying enough. My answer was not what she wanted to hear.

I didn't connect all those dots at that time but now know that I had been praying for myself whenever it was needed, but not in English. As I daily prayed in tongues, the Holy Spirit intervened for me countless times in countless situations and my natural understanding was totally disconnected from the process.

Throughout the epistles Paul makes several references to the importance of strengthening our inner being in order to finish our spiritual race. Just because you are born-again and Spirit-filled does not mean you have finished your race. Actually, those two experiences are only the beginning of an eternal relationship with God. I call my 'everyday tongues' my HGPS, my Holy Ghost Positioning System. He knows exactly where I am and where I should be at all times and will lead me there if I will simply follow Him. Believers need to be led by the Holy Spirit hour by hour, sometimes minute by minute, and consistently praying in tongues keeps us connected to our spiritual HGPS.

Both Paul and Jude tell us that the gift of speaking in tongues is given to edify and spiritually strengthen believers in Jesus Christ.

He that speaketh in an unknown tongue edifieth himself; but he that prophesieth edifieth the church (1 Corinthians 14:4).

But ye, beloved, building up yourselves on your most holy faith, praying in the Holy Ghost (Jude 20).

Praying in what I call 'everyday tongues' edifies and strengthens the one who is praying. Webster's Dictionary defines 'to edify' as to instruct or encourage, especially for moral or spiritual improvement. It also means to enlighten, educate and uplift. Surely you agree you need all of that you can get.

The word 'edify' may also be translated 'charge.' Praying in tongues is given as one of the tools to 'charge-up' and reinforce your spiritual being. Believers must be continually strengthened with might in our inner man:

That he would grant you, according to the riches of his glory, to be strengthened with might by his Spirit in the inner man (Ephesians 3:16).

A single charge is not enough. We need to be incessantly infused with the power of the Holy Spirit in order to live healthy, victorious, and successful lives here in the earth. Just like you would put a charge on a weak battery to build it up, you can build up your spiritual strength by praying in tongues. You can do this at will, any time, day or night. Praying in 'everyday tongues' is a tool of the Spirit given to help us accomplish that. If you are ill, weary, confused, oppressed or defeated your spiritual battery is weak and you can charge it up by praying in tongues. The primary purpose of our 'everyday tongue' in our personal lives is to strengthen us spiritually and awaken us to spiritual things.

One of the most important things you do when you pray in your 'everyday tongues' is build yourself up from the inside out and fortify your own soul and body. Primarily, praying in tongues strengthens your faith in God and causes your natural man to be alert to spiritual things. Your spirit man, which is new in Christ, is already strong, but that strength needs to be translated to your natural man.

Therefore if any man be in Christ, he is a new creature: old things are passed away; behold, all things are become new (2 Corinthians 5:17).

Co-laboring with the Holy Spirit by praying in "everyday tongues" transfers the life from your strong spirit being to your mind, will and emotions and brings wholeness to your physical body.

You are already whole in Christ. The condition of our triune being is dictated by the strength from within our spirit man communicating to our outer man. If you are sick, weak, confused or depressed, you are not connecting with your whole and healthy spirit man. Co-laboring with the Holy Spirit by praying in your 'everyday tongues' transfers the life from your strong spirit being to your mind, will and emotions and brings wholeness to your physical body. That is a fixed law of God and never changes. When you allow your spirit man to rule, your mind becomes clear and focused, and your body becomes strong. The power of that connection cannot be underrated. Life becomes sweet and successful.

If believers are to be all God has called us to be and receive all that He has provided for us to have, our spirit, soul and body must be continually edified. That doesn't happen automatically. Believers can never live in the fullness of the abundant life Jesus died to give us without strengthening ourselves in Him on a regular basis. Edifying yourself should be a definite priority in your life. We need to be renewed day by day, and we can do that by praying in our 'everyday tongues.'

> For which cause we faint not; but though our outward man perish, yet the inward man is renewed day by day (2 Corinthians 4:16).

You must discipline yourself to pray in tongues regularly. You cannot help others if you are defeated yourself so, if you want to be a blessing to others, put your own oxygen mask on first. Consistently strengthening and invigorating your soul and body by praying in your 'everyday tongues' keeps you prepared to be an extension of Jesus to those who are hurting.

> But you, beloved, building yourselves up on your most holy faith, praying in the Holy Spirit, keep yourselves in the love of God, looking for the mercy of our Lord Jesus Christ unto eternal life (Jude 20-21 NKJV).

Jude reinforces what Paul taught; a person who prays in an unknown tongue builds and edifies himself. Again, we see that speaking in tongues fortifies our God-given measure of faith and keeps us anchored in the love of God.

For I say, through the grace given unto me, to every man that is among you, not to think of himself more highly than he ought to think; but to think soberly, according as God hath dealt to every man the measure of faith (Romans 12:3).

Keep yourselves in the love of God, looking for the mercy of our Lord Jesus Christ unto eternal life (Jude 21).

The Greek words translated 'building yourself up' more accurately mean 'to construct.' As referred to in Jude 20, praying in your heavenly language is a construction project. As you pray in tongues, you build and reinforce your faith and strengthen your inner man. You can also construct a barrier around your soul (your mind, will, and emotions) to prevent the enemy from deceiving you. Praying in tongues releases to your physical body the healing virtue of Jesus already resident in your spirit man. If you are sick, depressed, or discouraged, I believe that can be rectified by properly utilizing the gift of tongues God has given you. When we find ourselves in places of defeat we need to recognize that we are not co-laboring with the Holy Spirit and take our tongues off cruise control. Using our *power tools* establishes the spirit man's place of authority and helps bring the carnal man and physical body into submission. Learn how to work with the Holy Spirit and He WILL build you up from the inside out.

Purposefully using the gift of tongues keeps our heart connected to the power of God. Love is God Himself and the very essence of His being. His power is love. God's love for mankind never changes. He will never leave us, and nothing can cause His love for us to fail; but, we can disconnect from that love. Our life choices draw us closer to God, or further away from Him. Speaking in our 'everyday tongues' is a choice we make to yield to the Holy Spirit, and He always draws us to God and keeps us connected to Him and His immense love for us.

Praying in tongues doesn't give you faith. Faith comes by hearing the Word of God: '*So then faith cometh by hearing, and hearing by the word of God*' (Romans 10:17). But praying in tongues does build you up on the measure of faith already given to you by God:

> For I say, through the grace given unto me, to every man that is among you, not to think of himself more highly than he ought to think; but to think soberly, according as God hath dealt to every man the measure of faith (Romans 12:3).

Praying in your 'everyday tongues' equips you to see the situations in your life as Jesus sees them. It exposes the enemy so you can see his strategies far off. From God's viewpoint, everything you face is trivial because the price has already been paid, and the war has already been won. There is always a place of triumph in Christ for the believer, and the Holy Spirit knows the way of escape.

> Now thanks be unto God, which always causeth us to triumph in Christ, and maketh manifest the savour of his knowledge by us in every place (2 Corinthians 2:14).

Even though deliverance from difficult trials is available to you, the exit sign you need to find could be completely blurred from your sight. You need clear spiritual vision to find that exit, and you can access that vision by using your *power tools*. Tongues opens our spiritual hearing and sight to God's Kingdom and can provide the vision and understanding we need.

I'll discuss more of the benefits of praying in our 'everyday tongue' in Chapter 11.

CHAPTER 9

WORKING WITH THE HOLY SPIRIT

And I will pray the Father, and He will give you another Helper, that He may abide with you forever— John 14:16

I love this verse; it is so full of promise! I particularly like to read it in the Amplified Version of the Bible. The word 'Helper' is explained and we see a bigger picture of the nature and work of the Holy Spirit.

And I will ask the Father, and He will give you another Comforter (Counselor, Helper, Intercessor, Advocate, Strengthener, and Standby), that He may remain with you forever— (John 14:16 AMPC).

This is so exciting and encouraging! Jesus promised to send us help, and He kept His word. Everything Jesus died to give us, and everything we will ever need while we live on earth, is already available and at our ready access through the Holy Spirit. He will lead us, counsel us, help us, intercede for us and do everything necessary to carry out the provisions of the Covenant on our behalf IF we will work with Him. The Holy Spirit is our helper; He is not our servant. Understanding that is a major key to apprehending spiritual things. The Holy Spirit undergirds and strengthens our faith, but it is entirely a matter of personal choice to use our faith and work with Him to accomplish the Father's will in our own lives and in our sphere of influence. To effectively use our gift of tongues, that great *power tool* of the Spirit, we must learn how to honor, listen to, yield to and cooperate with the Holy Spirit.

When we as believers pray in tongues, we move into a deep and profound communion with God that cannot be accessed by praying in our native language. I believe that an ignorance of the use of the gift of tongues has cost the Body of Christ dearly and I urge you to decide that you won't be like others who leave this precious gift an untapped well of promise. I am convinced that failure to engage with the Holy Spirit while using our gift of tongues significantly contributes to believers failing to receive and enjoy wholeness. Our Covenant with Jesus Christ provides us health, prosperity, peace, joy and so much more and we should desire to possess all that our good and gracious heavenly Father has given us through His Son. I trust that the understanding you're receiving in this book is already stirring your well of living waters and awakening you to anticipate change in your life.

In this chapter, we are going to take a look at what it means to work with the Holy Spirit.

It is fully God's will for all His children to possess every-thing that Calvary and the resurrection of Jesus provided; but, you don't have to look any further than your own life to see that the bountiful covenant blessings promised by God are not man-ifesting to the degree they are promised in the Scriptures. The majority of the Body of Christ is not enjoying the abundant life Jesus died to give us:

> The thief cometh not, but for to steal, and to kill, and to destroy: I am come that they might have life, and that they might have it more abundantly (John 10:10).

I believe that by actively working with the Holy Spirit we can begin to see our covenant provisions become a reality in our lives.

> For we are labourers together with God: ye are God's husbandry, ye are God's building (1 Corinthians 3:9).

> We then, as workers together *with Him* also plead with you not to receive the grace of God in vain (2 Corinthians 6:1 NKJV).

We are workers together with the Holy Spirit. He longs for the Church to receive all the manifestations of God's grace and knows we cannot do that alone. The Holy Spirit is with us and in us, '*even the Spirit of truth; whom the world cannot receive, because it seeth him not, neither knoweth him: but ye know him; for he dwelleth with you, and shall be in you*' (John 14:17) and wants to help all believers live victorious and fruitful lives. I am fully persuaded that before we can experience victory we must first learn how to yield to Him. The gift of tongues is given as a tool to empower the believer to bring the Kingdom of heaven to earth; and, one of the best ways I know to do that is to actively engage with the Holy Spirit in my heavenly prayer language. All believers need to know how to hear the Holy Spirit and follow His lead. That takes time, training and discipline. For me, the easiest way to do that is to quiet my soul and pray in tongues.

> And they went out and preached everywhere, the Lord *working with them* and confirming the word through the accompanying signs. Amen (Mark 16:20 NKJV).

Just as Jesus worked with His disciples while they co-labored with Him on the earth, the Holy Spirit works with believers today. Jesus sent our 'Helper' for that purpose. There is so much available for the Body of Christ, but few receive the riches of heaven in a tangible form. We must be taught the dynamics of working with the Holy Spirit in order to see heaven's provisions released as tangible realities in our lives. Bringing heavenly things to earth is a co-laboring project, and I find that sometimes believers fail to understand this principle. Again, the Holy Spirit is not our servant; we are co-laborers with Him. He works with us to bring heaven to earth but He doesn't do all the work for us. Merely standing on the sidelines hoping the Holy Spirit will automatically bring us all we need is not scriptural and will not produce the results we need and expect.

> Just as Jesus worked with His disciples while they co-labored with Him on earth, the Holy Spirit works with believers today. Jesus sent our 'Helper' for that purpose.

All believers need to know how to partner with the Holy Spirit and using the gift of tongues helps in that process. When you use your spiritual language, you verbalize divine things that will change you and change your world. Praying in tongues gives believers access into the heart and will of God. By connecting faith and tongues together we can release and transport the provisions of heaven. The language itself is a force that carries the life of God wherever it goes. It releases the power and presence of God like a heat-seeking missile into our lives and into situations and the lives of others.

For we are His workmanship, created in Christ Jesus for good works, which God prepared beforehand that we should walk in them (Ephesians 2:10 NKJV).

Believers are created to do good works. How can we ever expect to do good works of any kind or enjoy the fruit of those works on our own merit? We can't; our humanity is greatly flawed, but by co-laboring with the Holy Spirit we can do everything our loving heavenly Father requires of us. I may sound like a worn-out record but I cannot stress strongly enough the importance of learning how to work with the Holy Spirit. It is a definite necessity for us. Perhaps you have heard the old adage, 'Salvation is free, but maintaining it costs you everything' (unknown author). Part of that cost is laboring by faith with the Holy Spirit. No one gets saved and then lives the remainder of his life in bliss with no effort on his part.

I believe the best way to work with the Holy Spirit is by praying in tongues, but just going through the motions is not enough in and of itself. It is possible to speak in tongues every day of your life and still be very carnal and often defeated. That was my experience for the first twelve years after my salvation, but it certainly wasn't God's plan for my life, and it isn't His plan for your life, either. I took many wrong paths and had many failures during those early years that I now know could have been avoided if I had only known then what I know now about the value of using my gift of tongues to work with the Holy Spirit.

Jesus gave us the Holy Spirit to teach us truth and lead us into victory, but His intervention in our lives is not automatic. I learned that the hard way and hope to spare you disappointment and a similar outcome. Until Spirit-filled believers learn how to cooperate with the Holy Spirit, we can go through all the motions of being a Christian and never see significant external changes in our lives. Our inner man is changed instantly at salvation, but the external things that affect our everyday lives are changed through an ongoing working relationship with our 'helper,' the Holy Spirit.

How do you begin a working relationship with the Holy Spirit? You begin by asking.

> Yet ye have not, because ye ask not. 3 Ye ask, and receive not, because ye ask amiss, that ye may consume it upon your lusts (James 4:2b-3).

We receive everything from God the same way; first we ask, and we ask for the right reasons. One of the ways we ask amiss (ask out of a wrong heart motive) is by asking God to do everything for us. In a sense, that would be spiritual welfare. With that kind of mindset, we can unknowingly take on a false sense of entitlement that will never produce anything but doubt and confusion. I have met many a weary saint who has been doing nothing for decades but wait on God to do something in his life. They believe that someday soon God will _____ (fill in the blank), but nowhere in Scripture does God say that He's the 'Great I'm going to be.' He is the great I AM. Now is the day of our salvation.

> For he saith, I have heard thee in a time accepted, and in the day of salvation have I succoured thee: behold, now is the accepted time; behold, now is the day of salvation (2 Corinthians 6:2).

Faith requires both love and works to make heavenly things tangible.

> For in Jesus Christ neither circumcision availeth any thing, nor uncircumcision; but faith which worketh by love (Galatians 5:6).

> But wilt thou know, O vain man, that faith without works is dead? (James 2:20).

One way we receive from God the natural things we need to live our everyday lives is by working with the Holy Spirit to see them become living realities. Praying in tongues is not the only way to work with the Holy Spirit, but I find it to be the most efficient.

The gift of tongues is both a tool and a weapon but doesn't manifest as either until we yoke with the Holy Spirit and work with Him. He has the power and we must ask the Holy Spirit to mentor us and then choose to cooperate with Him in order to avail ourselves of the glorious provisions of our covenant with Christ. The Holy Spirit is waiting for that invitation. Ask Him right now. 'Holy Spirit, please help me. Show me Jesus and reveal to me things I cannot see. Teach me how to work with You.'

That which I see not teach thou me (Job 34:32a).

How do you work with the Holy Spirit? Co-laboring with the Holy Spirit means that we purposefully listen to Him as He gives us direction, insight, discernment or wisdom from heaven. When He speaks to us, He also equips us to do whatever is necessary. Praying in tongues initiates that interaction and makes it possible for us to clearly see, hear and know spiritual things. Once we see and know the plan of God, the Holy Spirit also equips and empowers us to respond appropriately. If you commit to work with the Holy Spirit, soon, even the most difficult situations will no longer appear impossible. Sometimes, He will lead you to declare something from the Word of God. Sometimes, He will require a specific action; sometimes He wants you to worship; sometimes He wants you to rest. Regardless of the instruction, listening and obeying is your part in the co-laboring process. Once you understand this interaction, you'll begin to see that everything becomes a 'fixed race.' The Holy Spirit will never tell you to do something without giving you everything you need to accomplish what He asks.

> If you commit to work with the Holy Spirit, soon, even the most difficult situations will no longer seem impossible.

Much of the supernatural is missing in our churches today and I believe that can be largely attributed to the fact that so few believers know how to yield to the Holy Spirit and follow Him. He longs to minister to the Church so that, through committed and submitted believers, Jesus can be lifted up and made clearly seen in the earth.

There are progressions we make in our walk with God. Every person who by faith acknowledges that Jesus Christ is the risen Son of God and accepts Him as Lord of his life becomes a child of God, *'For ye are all the children of God by faith in Christ Jesus'* (Galatians 3:26). However, there is a distinct difference between a young child and an heir: *'Now I say, That the heir, as long as he is a child, differeth nothing from a servant, though he be lord of all'* (Galatians 4:1).

As joint heirs with Christ, we must grow in Christ to become heirs of His Kingdom. An heir has tangible possession of, and full access to, the wealth of his father.

And if children, then heirs; heirs of God, and joint-heirs with Christ; if so be that we suffer with him, that we may be also glorified together (Romans 8:17).

We must develop into manifested sons so we can demonstrate the wealth of our Father's immense goodness. With earnest expectation, all of creation awaits the manifested sons of God.

For the earnest expectation of the creature waiteth for the manifestation of the sons of God (Romans 8:19).

These manifested sons are believers that do the 'greater works' Jesus said we could do.

71

Verily, verily, I say unto you, He that believeth on me, the works that I do shall he do also; and greater works than these shall he do; because I go unto my Father (John 14:12).

I am confident that these manifested sons of God are mature, submitted, and committed believers who co-labor with the Holy Spirit to bring heaven to earth. I encourage you to not limit God, but rather set your sights higher, and ask the Holy Spirit to develop you into an heir that demonstrates the majesty of the Father to the world.

To be established in Christ and live stable and victorious lives, each believer must daily consume God's Word and ask the Holy Spirit to reveal its truths. Simply reading God's Word like you might read a novel is usually unfruitful. The number one way God speaks to His children is through His Word. The Word of God lights our paths. *'Thy word is a lamp unto my feet, and a light unto my path'* (Psalm 119:105).

Head knowledge of the Bible has very little value; it is revealed knowledge we should seek. The Holy Spirit is the author of the Bible and only He can teach us the truths of the Scriptures from the inside out. I have discovered that one of the best ways for me to receive and retain revelation from my Bible is to read it while praying in tongues. If I find a passage difficult to understand, I'll reread it several times praying in tongues and the One who wrote it teaches me what I need to know. The Revelator makes God's Word a living epistle to me.

I depend upon the Holy Spirit to make the Scriptures come alive in me and often read my Bible while praying in tongues.

Tongues will release revelation to your natural understanding that you will receive by no other means. For me it's not quantity but quality that counts here. I have found that even ten minutes in the Scriptures while praying in tongues can profoundly impact my entire day. Often verses I've read many times before take on new meaning and life. Praying in tongues often causes me to see things I have missed before and causes them to awaken me to something new. I've also discovered that I always have better recall if I pray in tongues while reading the Scriptures. Jesus said that the Holy Spirit will bring to our remembrance what He has told us:

> But the Comforter, which is the Holy Ghost, whom the Father will send in my name, he shall teach you all things, and bring all things to your remembrance, whatsoever I have said unto you (John 14:26).

Reading your Bible with your *power tools* is a great way to co-labor with the Holy Spirit, and I trust you'll take advantage of this great tip.

Just as resistance training will build your natural muscles, praying in tongues builds your spiritual muscles. It's like working out with a personal spiritual trainer. Praying in tongues builds your spiritual strength. Your natural man will always yield to your carnal nature. Praying in tongues helps you bypass and/or resist that natural, innate tendency and enables you to refuse your carnal nature the right to get involved in your prayers. The more you pray in tongues, the weaker your carnal nature becomes. Working out with the Holy Spirit by praying in tongues pushes your natural weaknesses aside and brings the strength of your born-again spirit man to the forefront.

The Holy Spirit is a life source. When I exercise my faith and give preeminence to His leading in my life, I am propelled by and sustained in His strength. As I draw near to Him, the Holy Spirit draws near to me and I just yield to Him. Give the Holy Spirit His due place in your life and He will strengthen you and take you further in the things of God's Kingdom than you could ever go alone. Simply relinquish control and let Him take the lead. I see it somewhat as two professionally trained and highly skilled dancers on the dance floor. One takes the lead and the other follows in flawless and precise rhythm. The two literally move as one. It is the same thing in the Spirit realm when you allow the Holy Spirit to lead your life. I have found that consistently praying in tongues is the number one way to give the Holy Spirit His rightful lead in my life. Tongues bypasses our mental faculties and causes our faith to work effortlessly in the unseen. It's really not complicated.

Several years ago, the Lord told me that He had equipped me to, 'Send My dominion traveling,' and I have discovered that praying in tongues is the greatest tool I have to accomplish that. In Christ, through the power of the Holy Spirit, we are not limited to time or space. As we pray in tongues, we can be in more than one place at a time and, as we co-labor with the Holy Spirit, we can accomplish numerous things at once. In tongues, I can pray for multiple people and various situations all over the world all at the same time. It is impossible for me to cover that much territory in my native language, but working with the Holy Spirit in prayer has taught me that He is the ultimate multi-tasker and is unlimited in His ability. He is indeed my helper to bring the Kingdom of heaven to earth in my life and in the lives of those for whom I'm called to pray. I just need to be willing to work with Him to accomplish that.

The Holy Spirit always prays out the perfect will and plan of God: '*And he that searcheth the hearts knoweth what is the mind of the Spirit, because he maketh intercession for the saints according to the will of God*' (Romans 8:27). Whether I am praying for myself or for another I have great peace in knowing that, when I pray in tongues, my will and emotions are not getting in God's way. When I pray in English it is easy for me to allow my personal agendas and opinions to formulate my prayers. I can allow what I know naturally about the situation to lead me, but in tongues that is impossible. The prayers you pray in tongues are always in alignment with the perfect will of God and are pure and filled with life.

I have come to know that there are few things more rewarding than the Holy Spirit giving me an unction and the anointing to pray, and then yielding to that call. In those times I often have no idea what I'm praying about, especially when interceding for another person. Sometimes I don't even know who I'm praying for, but that doesn't seem important either. By praying in tongues, I take hold with the Holy Spirit and co-labor with Him to change, rearrange or remove things that are out of order. Every believer has this same privilege.

The Holy Spirit is continually looking for willing partners and I make myself available for those opportunities.

Mankind is created from the dust of the earth and there are things of heaven God wants to release in us, so we can release them to the world. We have no natural knowledge of these things, and no natural ways to access them.

Thy Kingdom come, Thy will be done in earth (mankind), as it is in heaven (Matthew 6:10).

I am fully persuaded that Kingdom business on that level is only accomplished by the Holy Spirit working with believers in the earth. I know of no other way to gain a natural understanding of those unknown things, or the knowledge of how to release them in the earth except by praying in tongues and co-laboring with the Holy Spirit, listening to Him intently with a determination of heart to follow His lead.

When God calls you to pray, or you simply have a desire to pray, never try to figure out in your head how to pray, just be grateful that the Holy Spirit knows everything and submit your spirit man and gift of tongues to Him. The primary role of the Holy Spirit is to glorify Jesus in the earth: *'He shall glorify me: for he shall receive of mine, and shall shew it unto you'* (John 16:14), and He knows how to perfectly do that in every situation. He will formulate the perfect prayer, and, as you submit to His lead, He will work to make Jesus seen in those areas. The outcome of every prayer the Holy Spirit prays lifts up and glorifies Jesus.

Speaking in tongues is a ***power tool*** given to the Body of Christ, both individually and corporately, to enable us to experience as a daily, tangible reality the Kingdom of heaven manifested in our lives here on earth. Speaking in tongues is not a stand-alone activity. The Holy Spirit, the Revelator, yearns to work with submitted and committed Christians to reveal Christ and release the power of heaven to earth that Jesus may be plainly seen and glorified. We need to know how to work with the Holy Spirit.

CHAPTER 10

INTERPRETING YOUR OWN PRAYER LANGUAGE

Wherefore let him that speaketh in an unknown tongue pray that he may interpret. For if I pray in an unknown tongue, my spirit prayeth, but my understanding is unfruitful. – 1 Corinthians 14:13-14

The word 'pray' in this passage means to petition or make a request. Here Paul instructs us to ask the Holy Spirit to interpret what we pray in tongues in a way that our human understanding may be fruitful.

In context, Paul refers to interpreting tongues that are given as a ministry of prophecy to a corporate body of believers. Perhaps you have witnessed the ministry of tongues and interpretation in your church services. These are valid gifts of the Spirit:

To another the working of miracles; to another prophecy; to another discerning of spirits; to another divers kinds of tongues; to another the interpretation of tongues (1 Corinthians 12:10).

Interpretation is imperative in a corporate setting because no one understands what is spoken, but interpretation is also necessary in your personal prayer language as well.

For if I pray in an unknown tongue, my spirit prayeth but my understanding is unfruitful (1 Corinthians 14:14).

Speaking in an unknown tongue and having no connection with what is spoken can be unproductive for the one who prays.

Tongues and the interpretation of tongues are gifts of the Holy Spirit. They are both something the believer must ask for and receive by faith. You receive the gift of interpretation the same way you received the baptism of the Holy Spirit and the gift of tongues; you ask and receive. Tongues is a tool that connects our human spirit to heaven, and we do not need to be ignorant bystanders in what God does in and through us. When we pray in tongues, it is sometimes appropriate and important to ask and believe God for a natural awareness of what we have prayed because the human intellect is totally disconnected from the spiritual realm. The only way we can know what we have prayed is by asking the Holy Spirit for an interpretation of the dialogue our spirit man has had with Him. That interpretation

> Tongues is a tool that connects our human spirit to heaven, and we do not need to be ignorant bystanders in what God does in and through us.

doesn't always come in words; it is usually comes as an impression or a deep 'inner knowing.'

Many Spirit-filled believers have never asked God to interpret to them what they pray in tongues. Why would you do that? When we pray in tongues, our spirit man that is one with Christ (1 Corinthians 6:17), communes with our all-knowing God. He alone has all wisdom and power and we need to know what He knows in order to live victorious lives in Christ. God alone possesses everything we require and longs to reveal to our understanding what we need in order to be more than conquerors in Him. *'Nay, in all these things we are more than conquerors through him that loved us'* (Romans 8:37). Only working with the Holy Spirit can make those victories a reality in our lives.

In your private devotional gift of tongues you can pray in your heavenly language at will, and as you mature in your relationship with Jesus, it should become commonplace for you to also request an interpretation of the Holy Spirit's directives to you. Praying in tongues and receiving interpretation is like turning on a light switch. What was dark or hidden can then be clearly seen. Praying in tongues releases things from a place deep inside you that cannot be accessed by natural means, and interpretation comes from your spirit man to your mind.

You do not need to be perplexed about what is happening when you use your *power tools*. By asking the Holy Spirit for an interpretation of your tongues, you can open yourself to a new walk with Him that is relational and deeply personal. The Holy Spirit truly longs for a relationship with the children of God. He has been given an assignment from Jesus to help us and He longs for fellowship, not a business arrangement, so I encourage you to talk to Him like a friend. Simply ask Him what you want and position your heart to receive. It will be a totally personal and private conversation because the language of the Spirit is completely concealed from the entire realm of darkness. The devil can never interpret our prayer language but, thankfully, we can.

When I need natural knowledge, the Holy Spirit releases it to me and makes the will of the Father known to my natural mind. I cannot pursue God's will if I don't know what that is, and I most often discover His plans for me while praying in tongues. I am not the only one who can do this; by faith, so can you!

My spirit being, filled with the Holy Spirit, knows all things, *'But ye have an unction from the Holy One, and ye know all things'* (1 John 2:20), and by praying in tongues and asking for an interpretation of what I have prayed, I can fully expect the wisdom of God to be revealed to my natural understanding. I can receive clarity and precise direction from God in countless situations by praying in tongues, but what good would that do me if I had no clue as to what I prayed or how the Father answered? Paul says that I can ask the Holy Spirit to interpret to my natural understanding what has been said, and I do that regularly.

For many Christians, praying in tongues becomes an occasional accessory rather than necessary and indispensable equipment. Some Spirit-filled believers in the Body of Christ go through the motions of speaking in tongues and never see any significant results from that heavenly communion in their own personal lives. Some of that can be remedied by asking the Holy Spirit to give you a clear understanding of the things you pray in tongues. Tongues is a commanding and useful *power tool* and, like any natural power tool, you have to know what the tool is designed to do and have good instruction on how to use it.

God frequently works through mankind and often the fruit of your prayers requires some active involvement on your part. You may need to make a natural connection to your heavenly language simply because there are things you need to do. Remember, you are co-laboring with the Holy Spirit, not coasting. You need to be a participator, not a spectator, in your prayers. When you pray in other tongues, you often connect with matters where you have no instinctive understanding and may need some level of interpretation to know exactly what natural things are required of you.

There are times that you will need no interpretation because God will use others to do the work and your prayers simply release the spiritual assistance they need. When I pray for an interpretation and do not receive one, I am often made aware that the latter is the case. I am simply co-laboring with the Holy Spirit to assist another who doesn't know how to do that for himself. The Holy Spirit often uses the 'buddy system,' and I've sometimes been made aware that another is picking up the slack for me. That is something the Holy Spirit does in His role as our Comforter. It is definitely comforting to know that someone else is praying when the situation you're in seems too overwhelming for you. It actually allows you to get your head above the murky waters and gives you hope.

The human spirit of a born-again believer in Jesus Christ is a deep well that is full of 'inside information.' Praying in tongues causes our natural intellect to connect with things our spirit man already knows but are obscured from our human understanding. The Holy Spirit lives inside the believer. He knows every mystery; nothing is hidden from Him. If we ask, He will not withhold from us what we need, when we need it. Things that are veiled can come into clear view when we pray in tongues and receive an interpretation of what we have prayed.

O Lord, I know that the way of man is not in himself: it is not in man that walketh to direct his steps (Jeremiah 10:23).

Man is not created to make his own way through life. We are surrounded by secular nonsense, and the ways of the world are continually drilled into us. The natural tendency of man is to follow after carnal ways and that never leads to a good outcome. *'For to be carnally minded is death; but to be spiritually minded is life and peace'* (Romans 8:6). One of the best ways to come out of the natural and into the spiritual is to pray in tongues. We need the Holy Spirit to instruct us on how to live Spirit-led lives in a carnal world, and one of the ways He does that is through an interpretation of our tongues. When praying in tongues our spirit man discusses divine mysteries with the Godhead and, through interpretation of our tongues, our natural minds receive divine instruction.

When you use your ***power tools,*** your spirit man often releases direction or revelation that has been previously veiled to your natural understanding. By asking for interpretation of your tongues, your spirit man will then translate to your understanding in your native language what you need to know as very clear thoughts to your mind. You will hear your own spirit man speaking to your soul. The gift of tongues is the tool that can release hidden information, and interpretation of your tongues can reveal to your natural mind what you need, precisely at the moment you need it.

When we trust the Holy Spirit and use our spiritual language, He releases His wisdom to our minds, and we receive vision and understanding we didn't have before. It has been my experience that praying in tongues actually makes me smarter. By asking for interpretation of what I have prayed in tongues, the Holy Spirit has revealed facts, figures, and details of situations where I had no natural knowledge or understanding. It is an amazing and humbling experience to be able to give correct answers and definitive information concerning matters where you've had no formal training. It's very easy to give all the glory to God in those situations because you are keenly aware that you have received divine assistance and are operating in nothing but the wisdom of heaven.

> Praying in tongues actually makes me smarter. By asking for interpretation of what I have prayed in tongues, the Holy Spirit has revealed facts, figures and details of situations where I had no natural knowledge or understanding.

I don't always ask the Holy Spirit to interpret to me what I am praying in tongues but, when I do, I often receive a response. Sometimes the interpretation comes as a knowing, and sometimes

I hear words in my spirit man. However the interpretation comes, along with it I receive a clear, natural understanding concerning my part in co-laboring with the Holy Spirit in that specific situation.

Here is an essential FYI (For Your Information); an interpretation of your tongues is not a translation, and it's important to understand the difference. A translation is a word-for-word retelling of something spoken. An interpretation is an overview or summary of something spoken. I don't believe the Holy Spirit has ever given me a word-for-word translation of what I have prayed in tongues, but He does give me an understanding of what I need to know. If I pray in tongues for 20 minutes and the interpretation that comes to me is only 30 seconds long, that doesn't concern me at all.

There are times I don't ask for an interpretation of my tongues because I have an inner witness, or what I describe as a 'deep knowing' about the essence of my prayer. Just yielding to that witness usually results in me receiving a very concise understanding of my part. Whether I receive an interpretation or not, I am definitely an active participant in my prayer in tongues, and the Holy Spirit often reveals to me things totally unknown to me.

I have come to know that I can pray in tongues at will, but I do not have that same luxury with interpretation. I don't believe I have ever experienced interpretation coming to me automatically. Even when I ask, the Holy Spirit doesn't routinely allow my understanding to know what I have prayed. I find that to be particularly true when praying for others. I often receive interpretation when it relates to me personally, but God is not in the gossip business and often conceals things from me when I pray for others. I believe interpretation of tongues is exclusively at the discretion of the Holy Spirit. It is a gift of the Holy Spirit and is given as He wills. I mention this because it is important that you not become discouraged if you do not receive an interpretation of your tongues every time you ask. You are in the heavenly army and just as it is in the natural military, you are usually on 'NTK,' a need to know basis. When you need to know, you'll know.

> But we speak the wisdom of God in a mystery, even the hidden wisdom, which God ordained before the world unto our glory: But God hath revealed them unto us by his Spirit: for the Spirit searcheth all things, yea, the deep things of God (1 Corinthians 2:7,10).

God often releases His wisdom in a mystery, and we need an interpretation of that mystery if it applies to our personal lives. Those mysteries are not hidden from us, but for us. Anytime you pray in tongues you can, and should, draw on the wisdom you are praying. By requesting an interpretation of your tongues, you invite the Holy Spirit to reveal to your understanding the deep things of God, especially as they relate to you personally. The Holy Spirit reveals the mysteries of heaven as they are relevant to you. That revelation may come by other means but often comes to your natural understanding through an interpretation of what you pray in tongues.

Part of the Holy Spirit's work is a 'construction project' in your inner man, and, if you'll ask, He will allow you access to interact with Him in the process. Praying in tongues awakens faith in you to release what is deep inside the well of your spirit man and the Holy Spirit will often reveal to you the building tools He is using to strengthen that faith. If you have never had the experience of interpreting your own tongues, follow Paul's admonition. He teaches us that we are to pray to interpret that our understanding may be fruitful. I encourage you to begin asking the Holy Spirit to interpret for you what you pray in tongues. Just ask and receive by faith. It really is just as simple as that.

...you do not have because you do not ask (James 4:2b NKJV).

Interpretation of tongues is not automatic. Again, you must ask for the ability to interpret your own tongues, or to have an awareness of what you have prayed. Just ask, and ask for the right reasons.

You ask and do not receive, because you ask amiss, that you may spend it on your pleasures (James 4:3 NKJV).

The Holy Spirit doesn't play games. He will not reveal the hidden things to indulge your carnal lusts or to give you fuel for gossip. The hidden things are revealed solely to accomplish God's plan, and carrying out His will must be our heart motive in asking for them. It is always for the Father's purposes that interpretation is given, and a great responsibility comes when you receive an interpretation of what you have prayed in tongues. Once revelation comes, you are responsible for it. Interpretation is almost always accompanied by an instruction and an assignment. When you receive instruction from the Holy Spirit you are then obligated, and also empowered, to do whatever is revealed for you to do.

Nothing in the Kingdom of God is complicated unless you make it that way. Your gift of tongues serves as a conduit to connect your spirit man to God. Your natural mind and body are both servants to your spirit man. Anytime you pray in tongues you can draw on the wisdom you are praying to direct, strengthen, or correct your natural man. The gift of interpretation is one way to help your spirit, soul, and body work together to do the good works of God.

> For we are his workmanship, created in Christ Jesus unto good works, which God hath before ordained that we should walk in them (Ephesians 2:10).

What can you expect when you receive an interpretation of your tongues? When you ask for an interpretation of your prayer language and allow your spirit man to yield to the Holy Spirit to receive, the voice you hear will sound like your own. You are simply yielding your gift of speech to the Holy Spirit and allowing Him to release utterances from your spirit.

> For he that speaketh in an unknown tongue speaketh not unto men, but unto God: for no man understandeth him; howbeit in the spirit he speaketh mysteries (1 Corinthians 14:2)

Your natural ears can hear what is spoken, but nothing in your natural man can interpret what is being said. It becomes somewhat like listening to a conversation on a party line, or for those of you too young to remember party line telephones, it's like being a part of a group chat. Through revelation or interpretation, our natural man receives understanding of the conversation.

When your mind hears the voice of God speaking from your spirit man it sounds like your own voice because it is your voice. The Holy Spirit uses your natural voice to speak in tongues, and interpretation comes the same way. Many miss an interpretation because they are expecting a supernatural voice to speak to them. The way an interpretation comes is supernatural, but the voice that delivers it is natural. It will come through an inner understanding or through something you say out of your mouth using your own natural voice. It will sound like you. It does take time and training to learn when your spirit man is talking and when you're just hearing your own human thoughts; but ask the Holy Spirit and He will surely help you identify the voice you are hearing.

> It does take time and training to learn when your spirit man is talking and when you're just hearing your own human thoughts; but ask the Holy Spirit and He will surely help you identify the voices you are hearing.

One way you will be able to discern the difference between an interpretation from the Holy Spirit and your own natural thoughts is to judge what you hear. A Godly interpretation will bring answers to your mind that you had not thought of or envisioned before. You will see or know things of which you have no natural knowledge. Remember, praying in tongues reveals the mysteries of God so, if you 'think' of things that describe a path you would normally take to resolve a matter, you most likely have not received an interpretation of your tongues, you have simply figured out something new on your own. You and I both know that natural reasoning rarely produces the highest and best result. In my experience, a true interpretation of tongues always reveals at least one previously unknown element to my natural understanding.

Interpretation of your tongues comes in many ways. You may receive a natural understanding immediately, but in my personal prayer life that is more rare than common. More often, after praying and asking the Holy Spirit to interpret my tongues, I will go on about my day and find that my understanding becomes illumined as I stay in faith to receive and maintain an attitude of thanksgiving and worship in my heart. Sometimes simple things like the words of a song or the headline in a newspaper or something printed on a billboard will trigger a release of knowledge I didn't have before. The natural thing is not the answer, it is just a trigger that awakens me to the answer. I then receive clear understanding concerning a certain matter of prayer and have a steady sense of assurance in my spirit man that my interpretation has come.

As a practical example of how a situation like that might happen, let's use the scenario of praying in tongues prior to going to a job interview. You have prayed about the job, are confident God has led you to it, and have asked the Holy Spirit to help you. You arrive at the interview and during the dialogue with your potential employer you are asked a question you cannot answer. You open your mouth to tell the interviewer that you are unable to answer that question but, instead, you give the perfect answer. The Holy Spirit is the Spirit of wisdom, and He will give you what you need to fulfill the plans and purposes of God. That could be a form of interpretation of tongues. When you prayed in tongues before the interview and activated your faith to receive, the Holy Spirit deposited the answer you needed in your understanding, and you were able to access it as necessary, not before. That is a very simple example, and that's my point. Interpretation of tongues comes in easy to understand ways.

Whether the Holy Spirit works with us in the simple things of everyday life or matters of greater importance with more complexity, He always requires our cooperation. Contrary to a teaching that is popular in some churches, you are not a passive bystander in your walk with the Lord. You are in partnership with the Holy Spirit to administrate the Kingdom of Jesus Christ in your own life. By praying in tongues, you can actively work with the Holy Spirit to bring heaven and earth together. God is not trying to make things difficult for us. The Holy Spirit will work in your personal life as much as you will allow Him. He is looking for willing partners, not forced laborers and, if you draw near to Him, He will take the lead. All natural flesh and things are subject to God and the more we willingly cooperate with the Holy Spirit, the quicker divine intervention can manifest on our behalf.

I Corinthians 14:15 asks, '*What is the conclusion then? I will pray with the Spirit, and I will also pray with the understanding. I will sing with the Spirit, and I will also sing with the understanding*' (NKJV). You can pray with your understanding. You can praise God with your understanding. You can sing with your understanding. And, you can do all of that at a higher level by doing it in tongues and asking for an interpretation.

I have many personal testimonies I could share about amazing results I have received through an interpretation of my own tongues, and also the tongues of others. One significant story involves the title of this book. In the beginning pages of this book I wrote a special thank you to Thelma Campbell. Thelma is a woman I know to have a strong and effective prayer life. She is a regular member of a prayer group that, at the time of this writing, I have co-led for over 18 years. Thelma is a charter member of that group and we have prayed together countless hours over those years.

I had begun writing this book but had laid it down numerous times, too distracted and too busy to finish it. I had written down a few possible titles for the book but wasn't satisfied with any of them. I was in a corporate prayer meeting where Thelma Campbell was present and she was praying firmly and boldly in tongues. I was nearby praying in tongues as well when I heard a crystal-clear English translation of Thelma's tongues. What I heard was so clear, for a moment I thought she was speaking loudly to me from across the room. I heard her call my name and she had my complete and undivided attention, but I quickly realized she was still praying in tongues and not talking directly to me at all.

This is what the Holy Spirit said to me through Thelma's tongues. He said, 'Linda, write; and this book will be called *Fire Up Your Power Tools*.' Every cell in my body heard every one of those words and as they were still echoing through my spirit I saw a quick picture in my mind of a man turning on a large power saw and cutting quickly and effortlessly through something impenetrable. There were white hot flames of fire shooting out from the blade as far as the eye could see. I was fully persuaded I had heard from God and from that day to this I have never debated what to title this book or that a chain saw belonged on the cover.

Looking back over the years, I can say that most of the critical, life-defining decisions I have made for myself or for my family have come as a result of spending dedicated time praying in tongues and asking for, and receiving, an interpretation of what I prayed. Because I keep myself stirred up on my holy faith, my spirit man stays primed to release a gusher of revelation when I need it most. Once I hear the Word of the Lord, I don't move off of it, regardless of what my natural eyes may see, or ears may hear to the contrary. None of that bears any weight with me at all. I know God has spoken and if I will cooperate with Him, things will manifest exactly as He says.

I encourage you to make a heartfelt commitment to respect your *power tools* and use them regularly. Never again take for granted the unlimited power that God has given so freely. Willingly interact with Holy Spirit, allow Him to lead you, and ask Him to interpret your tongues to your understanding. Draw near to Him and invite Him to sit in the driver's seat of your life. He will not do any of that automatically but, if you set your faith to receive spiritual insight from Him, you'll not be disappointed. I promise you, learning to interpret your own tongues will be a game changer in your relationship with your Divine Helper.

CHAPTER 11

EXECUTING KINGDOM PURPOSE

If you have ever questioned what you are doing when you pray in tongues, you are not alone, and help is on the way. We are going to look at some of the ways we use our *power tools* to co-labor with the Holy Spirit and also talk a little more about our 'everyday tongues.' When we pray in tongues, we do far more than fill the room with words. We make ourselves available to co-labor with the omniscient, omnipotent, all-powerful Holy Spirit to do something specific that glorifies Jesus and administrates or executes a Kingdom purpose.

Many believers coast along in tongues, but I encourage you to be a very active participant in your conversations with heaven. Trustfully, this chapter will help you understand how to better participate with the Holy Spirit as you pray on a level much higher than natural, cognitive ability. I hope to give you a good working knowledge of some of the specific things the Holy Spirit does in the earth. It will help you have a better understanding of what you can co-labor with Him to release into your personal life, into the lives of your family members and those in your sphere of influence, or into situations and lives where He may call upon you to pray.

As I previously mentioned, it is possible to speak in tongues and be completely ignorant of what you are doing. Our lack of knowledge doesn't always impede the Holy Spirit, but it definitely hinders our growth in God. Beginning on the day of my salvation, I embraced my gift of tongues and used it freely, but it was years later that the Holy Spirit began to lead my heart to explore the wealth of this gift. For several years I was faithful to pray in tongues as I was learning to walk with Jesus but was totally mystified about what I was doing and, quite frankly, didn't even have the wisdom or curiosity to ask. That seems so foreign to me now, but it was my reality then. Praying in tongues has always been a treasured gift to me and I honestly don't know why I didn't pursue knowing more about it. I have to rest in thinking that perhaps I simply wasn't ready for that knowledge, and the Holy Spirit spared me the anguish of possible confusion.

I pray in tongues continually; literally, all of the time. I have disciplined myself to pray in tongues nearly every waking moment that I am not eating or talking so I am praying in tongues many hours every day. Most of the time my praying is unpremeditated and somewhat casual. By that I mean I willingly engage my spirit man with the Holy Spirit and pray in tongues without the direct involvement of my heart or mind. I call that praying in my 'everyday tongues' or my maintenance prayers. Even though that form of tongues may appear to be casual on the surface, I've come to know that it is very powerful and effective. It produces a quickening to God and sharpens my awareness to spiritual things. It gives me both natural and spiritual strength and I'm made aware that my inner man is being fortified.

Praying in my 'everyday tongues' is much like natural, physical exercise. It keeps my spirit man strong, agile, and in shape for spiritual things. It keeps me responsive to the Holy Spirit, it builds my faith and keeps it active and alert.

> But ye, beloved, building up yourselves on your most holy faith, praying in the Holy Ghost, (Jude 20).

Praying in my 'everyday tongues' also brings a natural refreshing, somewhat like I might feel after a good physical workout. I am strengthened and renewed both spiritually and naturally when I pray in tongues.

I have also discovered that my everyday maintenance prayers in tongues give me a great gift. They enable me to pray into the future. The Holy Spirit is given to show us things to come. and will reveal those things to our understanding when we need them.

> Howbeit when he, the Spirit of truth, is come, he will guide you into all truth: for he shall not speak of himself; but whatsoever he shall hear, that shall he speak: and he will shew you things to come (John 16:13).

The Holy Spirit isn't constrained by time, and we can use our *power tools* to pray into the future. I have walked into countless situations over the years that could have become potential train wrecks. I would step into a big hot mess and be quickly made aware that I had already prayed into that moment. In an instant, my heart became illumined to the fact that I had at my immediate disposal all of the divine equipment necessary to experience a good outcome, and the knowledge of how to use it. I have often seen what could have become a disastrous situation appear as a blip on the radar screen and I have sailed right through circumstances that had serious complications for others. It was as if I were walking through hell in a bubble. I could see, hear and interact with everything going on around me, but none of it could touch me. In hindsight, I can see that everything I needed at that moment had been prepared for me as I prayed in tongues weeks or months or sometimes years earlier and was readily available the very instant the problem presented itself.

> By praying consistently in my 'everyday tongues', at the precise moment I have needed revelation about a situation, everything I required was already in my hand and at my ready access...

By praying consistently in my 'everyday tongues,' I have learned that, at the precise moment I have needed revelation about a situation, everything I required was already in my heart or in my hand and at my ready access to stop potential calamity in its tracks. I have learned that at the exact moment divine assistance is necessary, I can apprehend by faith all that has been prepared for me. Those are 'Happy Dance' times for me. Being able to dance over obstacles and assignments of the enemy is certainly much better than being crushed or stopped by them. Praying into the future is a glorious benefit of being well-trained in using your *power tools*.

Although praying maintenance prayers in tongues every day is good and even necessary, regularly praying with a specific objective is essential. Maintaining is good, but growing and moving forward is better; much, much better. If we only use the gift of tongues aimlessly and become content with using it solely for our personal benefit, I believe we'll miss much of the purpose and power in this heavenly tool. It is now common for me to regularly use my *power tools* for a specific purpose. In those times, I pray with a clear and explicit goal in mind. I lock in on a specific need and engage my heart and mind to hear from God. I pray with expectancy and employ my faith to see beyond this natural realm. Our *power tools* give us heavenly vision and enable us to see and hear heavenly things. They also stir within us a desire to give a response to the Holy Spirit which is a crucial and indispensable part of the co-laboring process.

When we pray in tongues, we willingly yield the heart of our spirit man and our natural tongue to the Holy Spirit and allow Him to speak to our Father God and/or God the Son using our human voice. It's a spiritual language, but our natural voice. We speak things that our natural mind does not know. The Holy Spirit uses our natural voice to connect with the heart and will of God and then speaks back to us the Father's instruction, correction, or direction. The Holy Spirit may also give us a spiritual supply like His vision to see the situation differently or a download of mercy. Your conversations in tongues are like an encrypted code and cannot be understood by the enemy or any force of darkness. It sounds like scrambled garble to them. You can pray out a multitude of secret things in your heart in tongues, and the enemy will have no access to what you pray.

We are very weak in our humanity, and the Holy Spirit intercedes for us when we don't know how to pray.

> Likewise the Spirit also helpeth our infirmities: for we know not what we should pray for as we ought: but the Spirit itself maketh intercession for us with groanings which cannot be uttered. And he that searcheth the hearts knoweth what is the mind of the Spirit, because he maketh intercession for the saints according to the will of God (Romans 8:26-27).

As you pray in your heavenly language, you work with the Holy Spirit to accomplish the Father's will in the earth. To best understand how we work with the Holy Ghost as we speak in tongues, it helps if we first know the Holy Spirit's responsibilities in the earth. Jesus gives us a summary of the Holy Spirit's primary jobs in the earth. They are recorded for us in the book of John.

> Howbeit when he, the Spirit of truth, is come, he will guide you into all truth: for he shall not speak of himself; but whatsoever he shall hear, that shall he speak: and he will shew you things to come. He shall glorify me: for he shall receive of mine, and shall shew it unto you (John 16:13-14).

According to these verses, the Holy Spirit's primary responsibilities are to:

- Guide believers in Jesus Christ into all truth

- Speak what He hears Jesus speak

- Show believers things to come

- Glorify Jesus

- Receive insight and instruction from Jesus and reveal it to His church

This short but power-packed list summarizes the heart of the Holy Spirit's assignments in the earth. These five things play out in innumerable ways, but everything the Holy Spirit does comes from this reservoir of grace and will always point to Jesus. Literally, our heavenly prayer language is a tool that allows us to work with the Holy Spirit in the earth to bring the will of the Father from heaven to earth. As we use our *power tools* to co-labor with the Holy Spirit, we work with Him and undertake a part of His mission to glorify Jesus and help His church. He helps us successfully navigate around, and sometimes through, the pitfalls of life.

I believe it is important for you to know what you are doing as you co-labor with the Holy Spirit praying in your heavenly language. Many have never asked what they're doing or given the matter any thought at all; but, I have come to know that it is VERY important to know what I am doing when I commit to purposefully pray in tongues. I want the Holy Spirit to show me the objective and my part in achieving that goal. Often, revelation concerning the end goal comes in parts but, when I ask what part I am to play today, the Holy Spirit always tells me my next step. I often receive just one instruction at a time and as I am faithful to follow through on that one, I receive more.

We don't work for God; we are workers together with Him:

For we are labourers together with God: ye are God's husbandry, ye are God's building (1 Corinthians 3:9).

We then, as workers together with him, beseech you also that ye receive not the grace of God in vain (2 Corinthians 6:1).

The member of the Godhead we co-labor with is the Holy Spirit, and one of the most efficient ways we do that work is by praying and engaging our *power tools*. To successfully co-labor with someone you both need to have the same goal. You may approach the goal differently and may have different assignments to achieve it, but to reach a productive and fruitful end result, everyone working on a project must have the same end goal in sight. That goal cannot be vague or confusing. The Holy Spirit will never give you an assignment that does not in some way glorify Jesus or help His church. It is easy to eliminate 'false assignments' that may rise up in your soul by keeping this truth in the forefront of your mind. It is so important you remember this that I'm going to say it again.

The Holy Spirit will never give you an assignment that does not in some way glorify Jesus or help His church.

If you are praying with no specific goal, you can expect to receive no specific result. This concept applies in all prayer. A great benefit to setting your heart to co-labor with the Holy Spirit as

100

you pray in tongues is that He defines the goal. You may think your goal is one thing when it may actually be something entirely different. I have often found that to be the case. What I naturally see or know about a situation is rarely the true heart of the matter, but the Holy Spirit who knows all things can show me what my human eyes do not see and my human understanding does not comprehend.

Praying in tongues is a relational, working arrangement. Tongues yokes you with the Holy Spirit to work on your behalf, or on behalf of others. When we pray in tongues, it is impossible to interject our personal agenda into the situation because we are co-laboring with the Holy Spirit to do something specific that He originates.

Below we are going to look at some of the things we can accomplish as we co-labor with the Holy Spirit in prayer. He works in limitless ways. I freely acknowledge that I am not presenting you an exhaustive list of all of the uses of tongues, but I do know this: as I pray in my heavenly language, I am fully aware that I am working in heavenly matters, and I'm definitely not working alone. I am working with the Holy Spirit to glorify Jesus in my life or in the life of another, or to help build or fortify His Church.

What Does the Holy Spirit Do?

If our prayers in tongues cause us to join the Holy Spirit on His assignments, the obvious question is this: "What does the Holy Spirit do?" Above, I've listed a summary of the Holy Spirit's jobs and below is a list of some of the countless, more specific ways He works in the earth. I have listed them in the order they appear in Scripture and have compiled them in a manner to refer to you personally, but everything on the list applies to all mankind and to every situation. Again, this is not an exhaustive list, but a compact collection intended to help you see some of the things that you may yoke with the Holy Spirit to see accomplished in the earth. When you purposefully pray in tongues, you co-labor with the Holy Spirit to do one or more of the following things. As you pray, the Holy Spirit begins:

- To give you wisdom, understanding, knowledge and skill (Exodus 31:3, 35:31)

- To give words of prophecy (1 Samuel 10:6, 10; 1 Samuel 19:20; Joel 2:28; Luke 1:67; Acts 2:17; 2 Peter 1:21)

- To empower you to speak the Word of the Lord (2 Samuel 23:2)

- To give you breath (Job 27:3)

- To constrain you (Job 32:18)

- To give you wisdom, understanding, counsel, might, knowledge and the fear of the Lord (Isaiah 11:2)

- To give you rest and refreshing when you're weary (Isaiah 28:11-12)

- To lift up a standard against the enemy (Isaiah 59:19)

- To warn you of danger (Matthew 2:13)

- To cast out demons (Matthew 12:28)

- To bring you into healing, and deliverance (Luke 4:18)

- To comfort you (John 14:16, 26, 16:7; Acts 9:31)

- To dwell in you as truth. He is truth (John 14:17)

- To teach you (John 14:26; 1 Corinthians 2:13; 1 John 2:27)

- To bring to your remembrance the things Jesus said (John 14:26)

- To testify of Jesus (John 15:26)

- To convict you of sin and reprove you of righteousness and judgment (John 16:8)

- To guide you into all truth (John 16:13)

- To show you things to come (John 16:13; Acts 21:11)

- To glorify Jesus (John 16:14)

- To make the ways of Jesus clear to your understanding (John 16:15)

- To convict the world of sin, righteousness and justice (John 16:8)

- To give you power to become an effective witness of Christ (Acts 1:8)

- To give you utterance in tongues (Acts 2:4)

- To help you speak the Word of God with boldness (Acts 4:31)

- To give you specific instruction (Acts 8:29)

- To magnify God (Acts 10:46)

- To call and separate you to the work of the ministry (Acts 13:2; Romans 15:16)

- To give you direction (Acts 23:11)

- To fill your heart with the love of God (Romans 5:5)

- To free you from the laws of sin and death (Romans 8:2)

- To quicken your mortal body (Romans 8:11)

- To lead you into equal sonship with Jesus (Romans 8:14)

- To deliver you from the bondage of fear (Romans 8:15)

- To pray for you (Romans 8:26)

- To help you in your weaknesses (Romans 8:26)

- To pray God's perfect will when you do not know how to pray (Romans 8:26-27)

- To bear witness to the truth of Christ (Romans 9:1)

- To give you hope (Romans 15:13)

- To empower you to preach the Gospel of Jesus Christ with signs and wonders (Romans 15:19)

- To search the hidden things and reveal the hidden wisdom of God (1 Corinthians 2:10)

- To cause you to know the things given to you in God (1 Corinthians 2:12)

- To live in you (1 Corinthians 3:16)

- To wash, sanctify and justify you in Jesus (1 Corinthians 6:11)

- To give you spiritual gifts (1 Corinthians 12:8-10)

- To speak mysteries (1 Corinthians 14:2)

- To encourage and strengthen you (1 Corinthians 14:4)

- To help you give thanks well (1 Corinthians 14:17)

- To give a sign to the unbeliever (1 Corinthians 14:22)

- To give life to the Gospel of Jesus Christ (2 Corinthians 3:6)

- To give you liberty (2 Corinthians 3:17)

- To transform you from glory to glory (2 Corinthians 3:18)

- To seal you to the day of redemption (Ephesians 1:13, 4:30)

- To give you access to the Father (Ephesians 2:18)

- To strengthen your inner man (Ephesians 3:16)

- To unite you to the Body of Christ in peace (Ephesians 4:3-4)

- To sustain you in times of waiting (Galatians 5:5)

- To produce the fruit of love in you (Galatians 5:22-23)

- To help you share the Gospel with power (1 Thessalonians 1:5)

- To give you joy (1 Thessalonians 1:6)

- To assist you in praying without ceasing (1 Thessalonians 5:17)

- To help you retain what you receive from God (2 Timothy 1:14)

- To renew you (Titus 3:5)

- To help you obey truth (1 Peter 1:22)

- To cause you to prophesy (2 Peter 1:21)
- To build you up on your most holy faith (Jude 20)
- To speak to you (Revelation 2:7)
- To call for Jesus' return (Revelation 22:17)

As you pray in tongues, you interact with the Holy Ghost and become a conduit to release a supernatural manifestation of one or more of these things listed above into your life, or into the life of another person or situation. **THAT** is what you do when you use your *power tools* and co-labor with the Holy Spirit in tongues. Even though to your mind your words may seem pointless, your prayers in tongues are not mindless chatter; you are working with the Holy Spirit to bring divine assistance and provision to earthly things. You don't do the work, you simply make your faith available and become a channel for Him to work through. The Holy Spirit does the work and He always glorifies Jesus in the process. Everything the Holy Spirit does will have that same end result. He has no assignment that doesn't directly or indirectly reveal Jesus to you or to another and He always and only glorifies Jesus.

The list above is limited, but the power of the Holy Spirit is limitless. Which of the things on the list do you need to see manifest in your life right now? Life draws life and, as you engage with the life-giving power of the Holy Spirit, His life will overtake you and bring the provisions of heaven to you. Since all natural flesh and things are subject to God, you should desire to willingly cooperate with the Holy Spirit. He alone can cause these divine interventions to manifest on your behalf.

You are not a passive bystander in your walk with the Lord. I cannot emphasize enough the importance of understanding that you are in partnership with the Holy Spirit to administrate the Kingdom of the Father and execute His will in the earth. By praying in tongues, you can actively work with the Holy Spirit to bring heaven and earth together. If you will discipline yourself to use your *power tools* daily and make praying in tongues a purposeful, active part of your everyday life, you will become far more aware of God and His will for your life and become very sensitive to the leading of His Spirit. You will rarely miss Him, and the problems that arise in your life won't crush or defeat you. Commit to the process, and in a short time, just like the song says, your life will become "Sweeter and Sweeter as the Days Go By."

FIRE UP YOUR POWER TOOLS

CHAPTER 12

BE CONSISTENT

Pray without ceasing. – 1 Thessalonians 5:17

What is prayer? I like D.L. Moody's definition:

"Prayer does not mean that I am to bring God down to my thoughts and my purposes, and bend His government according to my foolish, silly, and sometimes sinful notions. Prayer means that I am to be raised up into feeling, into union and design with Him; that I am to enter into His counsel and carry out His will purposefully." ~ Dwight L. Moody

Many believers think that prayer is something they have to do to get God to act on their behalf. That's not true at all. Prayer is a gift of God's grace to us; it is simply an opportunity to converse with Him to learn of and cooperate with His will. Paul, the apostle, exhorts us to engage in that conversation without ceasing. That means to have a continuous heart-to-heart conversation with your creator. Your *power tools* can help you do that. Paul's exhortation to pray without ceasing didn't make much sense to me until I began to understand that I was already praying without ceasing by praying continually in tongues.

As I mentioned in an earlier chapter, as a baby Christian, I decided to discipline myself to pray in tongues as much as possible. After listening several times to a Marilyn Hickey teaching in which she said I could pray in tongues all the time, I was really motivated to learn how to do that and was fully convinced that I could. I've learned when passion comes, discipline is an automatic and I had a passion to pray in tongues all the time, so disciplining myself to do it was not a chore. I was really serious about praying in tongues all of the time.

From that day to this I have not stopped exercising my prayer language, and my *power tools* continue to expand. Today, I am so disciplined to pray in my heavenly language that I pray in tongues well over 80% of my waking hours and will sometimes awaken myself in the night praying in the Holy Ghost.

A conversation is a dialogue, not a monologue. Once I understood that, I no longer prayed in tongues without an awareness of God and a continual expectancy that He would speak back to me. By praying in tongues throughout the day, I have discovered that I really can have a perpetual, life-giving conversation with the Almighty God.

You can put your gift of tongues on mindless autopilot, or you can do something powerful with it. Your *power tools* will not work at their highest and best potential for you unless you put them to work. It's your choice, and I encourage you to engage your heart with the all-powerful, all-knowing Holy Spirit. The Holy Spirit is a gentleman and will never force you to pray in tongues or coerce you to work with Him in spiritual things. He invites and never commands. Sometimes He will prompt your spirit man to pray in tongues, but will always wait for your response. The Holy Spirit will give the invitation and then wait for you to agree to work with Him. You need to intentionally engage your free will and give Him permission to use your voice.

What is the number one key to successfully co-laboring with the Holy Spirit? Without hesitation, my answer to that is consistency. Consistency has undoubtedly been the primary reason there is substance to my relationship with the Holy Spirit and the reason I stand solidly in Him. Because I pray consistently in tongues, I have come to expect consistent results. By praying without ceasing in tongues, whenever I find myself walking into difficult situations, I become aware that prayer has preceded me and I anticipate a good outcome. Those are sweet and glorious victories! I think to 'pray without ceasing' is a directive every believer should take seriously, and I highly encourage you to discipline yourself to consistently pray in your heavenly language. You will begin to experience benefits your natural man may not comprehend, but I promise you'll enjoy the fruit.

If you are going to pray without ceasing, you need to make an intentional, conscious decision to do that. You must yield your free will to the will of the Father and allow the Holy Spirit to pray through you. He will never force you. Praying in tongues is an outflow of your surrendered human will. You either yield to the Holy Spirit, tell Him 'no,' or ignore Him; it is always your choice. The Holy Spirit will never pressure you to do anything. He is not an outlaw and doesn't ambush you and take over your speech. People who tell me they have absolutely no control over what or when they speak in tongues are really telling me that they are not praying by the Holy Ghost at all. The Holy Spirit is not a terrorist and He will not hijack you and force you to do anything, ever.

Sometimes when counseling weak and defeated Spirit-filled Christians I can trace at least a portion of their sorrow and loss to having received the gift of tongues but neglecting to use it. They find themselves in the middle of a pit that could have easily been avoided by engaging their *power tools* and keeping their spirit man alert. Often, simply encouraging people to commit to pray in tongues and make tongues a consistent and permanent part of their walk with the Lord brings clarity to the immediate situation and understanding on the next step that needs to be taken to turn their lives around.

You can never successfully resolve conflict when you're depressed, overwhelmed, confused, or afraid. Every decision you make in those circumstances is the wrong one. Purposefully co-laboring with the Holy Spirit as you pray in tongues, and actively engaging your faith to work with Him, usually eliminates those strangleholds of the soul and gives you clear spiritual vision. That probably won't happen the first three minutes you pray in tongues, but if you are diligent and consistent and will make an effort to pray from your heart in tongues, your understanding will be illumined to truth. You will see things that have been previously veiled to your understanding, and you will receive wisdom on how to make necessary changes. You didn't walk blindly into that mess, and you can't walk out of it blindly either. Using your *power tools* gives you vision and a plan.

God has already provided by grace everything we will ever need to live healthy, happy, productive and peaceful lives but we must appropriate those things by faith. Our faith is a positive response to the finished work of Calvary and our lives should be a continual conversation between God's grace and our faith. Praying in our heavenly language facilitates that conversation because it builds us up on our most holy faith: '*But ye, beloved, building up yourselves on your most holy faith, praying in the Holy Ghost*' (Jude 20). That faith is pure and unpolluted by natural reasoning and is always effective.

By intentionally engaging our heart and consistently praying in tongues we fire up our *power tools* to release to our natural understanding the wisdom needed for our next move. It also increases our faith to do whatever is needed to access God's grace for our situation, or a situation He has put in our heart. Every time you pray in tongues, grace and faith are working together. Grace is talking; faith is responding. Abundant grace is God's part and He makes it abundantly available to every believer. Sadly, His grace is not always accessed because we fail to engage our

> Praying in tongues also increases our faith to do whatever is needed to access God's grace for our situation, or a situation He has put in our heart.

faith to receive. Praying in tongues awakens and ignites our faith to successfully respond to God's grace more readily.

Yielding to the Holy Spirit can prevent us from being blind-sided or walking into something dark and unknown. He knows our future, and if we will be alert to His leading, He will always guide us in the right direction. That alone is so comforting and life-giving and is a strong motivation to pray without ceasing. When we put our *power tools* to work for us, the Holy Spirit prays out the plans and strategies of God for our lives. I know that to be true personally, and I also know it isn't the result of occasional, aimless praying. When I pray consistently in tongues, not haphazardly, but purposely praying in my 'everyday tongues' or yielding my heart to the Holy Spirit with specific purpose, I find that I can pray out my future in tongues and give God's plan for my life an avenue through which to flourish. His plans for me are solid and sure; '*For I know the thoughts that I think toward you, saith the* Lord, *thoughts of peace, and not of evil, to give you an expected end*' (Jeremiah 29:11). However, that doesn't mean I will ever find or understand them. I personally know far too many believers who are totally clueless about God's specific call upon their lives.

I encourage you to harness your carnal man and train yourself to surrender your free will to the Holy Spirit. Grant Him permission to pray through you without ceasing. Once you do that, it won't be long before you discover many sweet advantages, including being able to walk into difficult and trying circumstances and realize they're not as difficult as you may have expected. Your fortified faith will drive out fear and you will be able to apprehend your victory. Once you have disciplined yourself to use your **_power tools_** to pray without ceasing, you will often pray the answer before trouble arises and will discover that answers are overtaking the problem even before it comes into view. I know these truths as realities in my life. They are life-giving and life-sustaining and I trust that you will embrace them as your own.

'Praying in tongues equips us to pray for things
no one thinks to pray about or about which
no one knows how to pray.'
~ Kenneth E. Hagin

FIRE UP YOUR POWER TOOLS

CHAPTER 13

MAKING IT PRACTICAL

How Did I Do That?

The most important part of learning new things about God and your relationship with Him is learning how to make those things work for you in your personal life. Knowing the 'what' and not knowing the 'how' of spiritual things can be frustrating and is usually fruitless. 'Know how' in any area of life is valuable. It can actually be priceless. How many times have you paid someone else great sums of money to do things for you that you didn't know how to do? In both natural and spiritual things, the 'how' is far more important and valuable than the 'what.'

Sometimes we need simple, practical instruction on how to apply a spiritual principle in order to make it effective in our own lives. This chapter is designed to give you just that. I will share with you examples of how I might personally use the fundamental truths on using my *power tools* to co-labor with the Holy Spirit. My goal is to give you guidelines, not formulas, and

I encourage you to use them as such. Prayer is relational, not a routine or ritual. I encourage you to use these examples to open your heart and help you better understand how to develop your own communion with God. My intent is to give you a roadmap, not a doctrine. How I use my *power tools* is not designed to be a destination for you, just a little assistance to help you find your own place in prayer.

I find that the only people who don't benefit from following the Holy Spirit are those who don't want to. I have known Christians who live their entire lives and never make an effort to find that wonderful connection; some that I loved dearly have died never accessing what was readily available. The Holy Spirit is a very willing 'Helper' and will always do His part. If you don't make the effort to connect with Him, you won't be bothered with good results. You can continue through life the same way you've been going, but soon you'll lose all hope for a better future, and find yourself singing that old song, 'Que Sera, Sera, whatever will be,' or, you can follow the procedures and reap the benefits. It's your choice. I trust that you will invest your *power tools* to engage in a working relationship with the Spirit of Truth and Grace and give Him the opportunity He longs for to make your life rich and full.

The Holy Spirit Is Always Faithful

I try to live in a state of readiness and make myself available to the Lord. Because of that, I am sometimes alerted by the Holy Spirit to pray concerning situations unknown to me. When that happens, I rarely begin praying in my native language; I pray in tongues and just connect with the Holy Spirit and follow the direction He puts in my heart. He invites and I follow; I never try to lead that dance. I love those supernatural calls to prayer, but it is far more common that I will receive natural requests. I will receive a call, e-mail or text from someone asking for prayer. I can't follow the Holy Spirit if I'm leading, so I always begin by asking if I have a place in the situation. I want to pray fervent and effective prayers, so this has become a basic and elementary starting point for me. I have come to learn that just because there is a problem doesn't always mean I have an assignment from God to undertake that problem in prayer.

Before I learned how to hear and follow the Holy Spirit, I wasted a lot of time and effort 'trying' to pray. He would often tell me that I was asking the wrong question or heading in the wrong direction in prayer. Now, I ask Him before I begin if I have a part, and if so, to define my part and show me how I should pray. He is always faithful to lead me. A natural army never goes to battle without a strategy, and we shouldn't go to prayer without one either. I now know heavenly strategies only come by following the leading of the Holy Spirit. The key is to let Him lead and not try to drag Him into something you already have your heart wrapped around. You have to refuse your thoughts or emotions a right to interrupt. That's usually more difficult than it sounds, especially if the prayer need involves someone you love, but staying in your rightful place always produces the best results.

I don't take on every prayer need people want to give me but remain sensitive to what the Holy Spirit is entrusting to me. Once I am assured He wants me to pray for a need, I agree and will usually pray immediately. Years ago, I was deeply convicted about telling people I would pray for them and then never doing it. That was never my intent but if I didn't pray immediately sometimes days would pass before that need would come back to my remembrance. Often that was too late. Since then, when I receive a request to pray, I will pray in tongues immediately, asking the Holy Spirit if He wants me to co-labor with Him in that situation. If He tells me, 'No,' I ask Him to send another seasoned laborer and don't press the matter further. If He says, 'Yes,' I'll continue praying, yielding my heart and listening to His instruction. I can usually do all of that and go about all the normal activities of my day. Occasionally, I'll know that I am to stop and give my undivided attention to the matter, but that doesn't happen often.

I'll give you a fictitious example. Let's assume that I am asked to pray for Mary because she is bound with addictions and has overdosed on a narcotic drug. I'll first ask the Holy Spirit if I'm to pray for Mary, and in this example, He confirms yes, I am to pray. I will begin to pray in tongues, keeping my heart open to hear a specific word or an instruction. If I don't hear something in a few minutes, I might ask the Father to release the Holy Spirit to do one or more of the things listed in chapter 11. I will pray in line with what I know the Lord would want to do in Mary's life. Perhaps I would pray in tongues with my heart focused on Mary to experience the liberty of God and to be set free of those addictions; *'For the law of the Spirit of life in Christ Jesus hath made me free from the law of sin and death'* (Romans 8:2). Perhaps I would pray that He bring her healing and deliverance; *'The Spirit of the Lord is upon me, because he hath anointed me to preach the gospel to the poor; he hath sent me to heal the brokenhearted, to preach deliverance to the captives, and recovering of sight to the blind, to set at liberty them that are bruised'* (Luke 4:18).

Regardless of where I start, I keep my heart very open to a change of directions. I actually anticipate it. As I mentioned earlier, I often find that what my natural eyes see or ears hear is rarely the real problem. Frequently, what I see naturally, or have been told, is simply the fruit of something totally unseen. Things like addictions are rarely the true problem. They are often rotten fruit being harvested from rotten seed planted years earlier. Dealing only with the fruit of a problem is somewhat like putting a Band-Aid on an open, gaping wound. It may bring some slight, temporary relief but is basically useless.

Even if I begin my prayer by addressing the natural information, I do not set my attentions on what I know or have been told. If I get caught up in the natural situation and keep my mind focused on the addictions and the devastating outcomes they bring, I will often miss the subtle leading of the Holy Spirit redirecting my prayer to the real problem. It's only when we deal with the real problem that we get viable and lasting results. Instead of focusing on the problem, I focus on Jesus. He is the answer. My goal in prayer is to go to the root cause of the problem and co-labor with the Holy Spirit to arrest, remove and annihilate that source. I listen for the Word of God that the Holy Spirit wants released into Mary's life. He always uses the Word of God, and I am fully persuaded that *His Word knows what to do*. My job is to hear that Word and speak it in faith. It will then do what it is designed to do in Mary's life. Once God's Word is released by faith into a situation, the Lord will perform it, just like He promised; *'Then said the* LORD *unto me, Thou hast well seen: for I will hasten my word to perform it'* (Jeremiah 1:12). Prayer like that brings permanent results.

There is another great benefit to praying like that. I don't get caught up in drama and stress. When I keep my focus solely on my part in the situation, I am elevated way above the turmoil and my emotions don't influence my prayer. When Paul wrote that we have a seat in heavenly places, he meant it:

> And hath raised us up together, and made us sit together in heavenly places in Christ Jesus (Ephesians 2:6).

We fail to enjoy that place simply because we're too earthly minded. We have to renew our minds to be heavenly minded in order to take our place in Christ.

If I need to know something specific about Mary or her problem, the Holy Spirit is faithful to reveal it to me. I can then pray by the Spirit with my understanding. Paul made it clear that we can pray both with the Holy Spirit and with our natural understanding:

> What is it then? I will pray with the spirit, and I will pray with the understanding also: I will sing with the spirit, and I will sing with the understanding also (1 Corinthians 14:15).

When praying in tongues I often see the unseen, but when praying for others, it has been my experience that the Revelator seldom discloses hidden things and personal matters when they may have an adverse impact on my own life. Unless He is warning me of an upcoming problem, I am rarely privy to the sordid details of the lives of people close to me. He is not in the business of uncovering your nakedness just to satisfy my curiosity. There have been rare exceptions to that, but generally, I have limited awareness or no natural understanding at all of the deep workings of the Spirit in the lives of people I know personally, especially if those things will negatively affect me or my family.

There is a danger that sometimes comes with gratified curiosity. Seeing unseen things that could potentially hurt or confuse me in any way could easily taint my heart motives and render me nearly useless in prayer. I fully understand that. Pure heart motives are essential for effective prayer. Actually, it is refreshing to have no natural knowledge of what I'm praying about. If the Holy Spirit does reveal hidden things in my own life, or in the lives of those closest to me, by His grace I am emotionally removed from them; so, my soul doesn't get a vote and I can receive clear understanding of what I am to do with that information.

Whether I see the true, underlying dynamics of the natural problem in Mary's life or not, I can unite with the Holy Spirit and pray out such a critical situation while fully resting in God and trusting Him to do whatever is necessary to bring about a good outcome. I know that I am not the one doing the work. Grace has already done all that needs to be done. Calvary is a finished work. I am just using my faith and engaging my *power tool*s to come alongside the One who releases those things in the earth. In some ways, it is somewhat like I am simply echoing what He says and when His words are spoken in the earth, they take on tangible form. I trust that the essence of that last sentence does not escape you. It is the heart of effective prayer.

Saying exactly what the Holy Spirit says over Mary causes her life to take on His life and sets her free.

Healing

Knowing how to co-labor with the Holy Spirit in the area of healing is something every believer will need more than once in his lifetime. I would say that well over 75% of the requests I receive for prayer are for healing. An injured, diseased or infirm body never brings glory to anyone, ever, and certainly not to Jesus. He died an unspeakably cruel death so that you and I might be free from all torment, affliction, infirmity and disease. God is never the author of sickness and He never causes tragedy. He has already made provision for each of His children to live free of sickness and disease. I encourage you to believe what He says, and not what the world, or your own physical body tries to tell you. If you are older, reject the lie that you need to expect pain and illness. Aging is inevitable, but deterioration is under the curse and you have already been redeemed from the curse; *'Christ hath redeemed us from the curse of the law, being made a curse for us: for it is written, Cursed is every one that hangeth on a tree'* (Galatians 3:13).

There is no place in God's covenant for weak, deteriorating bodies. Expect that to be your reality and make it your confession that you refuse to deteriorate as you age. I say over myself that I am going to live long and strong and not die until I'm satisfied. It will serve you well to do the same thing.

In praying concerning sickness, whether for myself or another, I often begin by joining my heart in unity with the Holy Spirit asking the Father to bring wholeness to the person to the glory of Jesus; *'Whether therefore ye eat, or drink, or whatsoever ye do, do all to the glory of God'* (1 Corinthians 10:31). The Holy Spirit comes to glorify Jesus. That is His primary job in the earth. *'He shall glorify me: for he shall receive of mine, and shall shew it unto you'* (John 16:14).

If the Holy Spirit is on the scene, He is looking for ways to make Jesus plainly seen. Having any other agenda in praying for the sick can be praying with a wrong motive. If you are the one ill, you may want relief from the screaming pain or reversal in a negative report, but you can't make that the sole focus of your prayer. The Holy Spirit will never co-labor with self-centered, selfish prayers. Instead, ask for wholeness so your life can be a testimony of the goodness of God: *'I shall not die, but live, and declare the works of the Lord'* (Psalm 118:17). That's a prayer He can work with.

> If the Holy Spirit is on the scene, He is looking for ways to make Jesus plainly seen. Having any other agenda in praying for the sick can be praying with a wrong motive.

The position you come from when you pray for healing is crucial. You are not the sick trying to get well; you are the healed taking possession of the spoil Jesus gained for you in His resurrection.

...who forgiveth all thine iniquities; who healeth all thy diseases; He sent his word, and healed them, and delivered them from their destructions (Psalm 103:3,107:20).

If you come before the Lord with any other mindset, your prayers are tainted. Pray from the position of defending the wholeness Jesus died to give you for the purpose of your life being glorifying to Him and watch how quickly the Holy Spirit comes to your aid. He is 100% in agreement with that kind of prayer.

I know I'm preaching to the choir, but I must say again that asking God is an essential part of the process. It may seem very elementary but asking is the foundation of effective prayer. Regardless of what we pray for, we must first ask the Father according to His will, and ask with the right heart motives.

Ye lust, and have not: ye kill, and desire to have, and cannot obtain: ye fight and war, yet ye have not, because ye ask not. Ye ask, and receive not, because ye ask amiss, that ye may consume it upon your lusts (James 4:2-3).

Once we approach the Father in Jesus' name, we must ask Him what He wants accomplished in the situation.

And in that day ye shall ask me nothing. Verily, verily, I say unto you, Whatsoever ye shall ask the Father in my name, he will give it you (John 16:23).

Making His goal our goal always brings His help. I do that and then pray in my heavenly language, intently listening for an answer. I will pray in tongues a little, listening to my spirit man and then be quiet and wait for a response from the Holy Spirit. I don't do all the talking. This is a very important part of learning how to co-labor with Him. I learned a long time ago that what I have to say about a situation pales in comparison to what He has to say. It will go well for you to let the Holy Spirit do most of the talking. The most important part of prayer is listening so be sure to give the Lord time to speak when you ask.

Praying in tongues brings a rest and a refreshing; *'for with stammering lips and another tongue will he speak to this people. To whom he said, this is the rest wherewith ye may cause the weary to rest; and this is the refreshing: yet they would not hear'* (Isaiah 28:11-12). Co-laboring with the Holy Ghost is not laborious. When you're working with Him, your part of the load is light. If I'm praying and begin to feel weary or drained, I know I've stepped off God's ordained path somewhere and it is a clear sign for me to stop and recalibrate my course. I have met self-proclaimed 'intercessors' who look like they've been dragged behind a galloping horse. I've even had some tell me that the reason they look so bad is because they've been in spiritual warfare and were beaten up in prayer. That's a lie. If you believe that, you are greatly deceived. The war is over; you just need to come out of your foxhole.

When your ways please the Lord, He causes your enemies to be at peace with you. *'When a man's ways please the Lord, he maketh even his enemies to be at peace with him'* (Proverbs 16:7). Even if the situation is desperate, there is no drain of your natural strength when you are co-laboring with the Holy Spirit; but, I can tell you from experience that great weariness will accompany works done in the flesh. Those works will not only defeat and deplete you now, but will burn on the day of reckoning, producing nothing now, and nothing then. Weariness of your flesh in seasons of prayer is a flashing red light to stop. Take a deep breath and rest in the finished work of the cross.

Complete rest is the most common recommendation doctors give to someone who is seriously injured or gravely ill. Using your *power tools* can bring a refreshing to your spirit man and cause you to experience genuine inner peace. The human body has the God-given capability to heal itself and often needs only total rest to facilitate that healing. Praying in tongues brings rest, genuine rest; it brings a deep, recuperative rest to the inner man. It brings the Shalom of God. Praying in tongues can release healing to your body. It releases strength to your soul and physical flesh. I have experienced that during times of illness. By yielding to my gift of tongues, I have tangibly entered into the rest of the Lord and experienced it bringing a revitalizing and restorative rest that comes from the inside out. I just pray in tongues with my heart and mind focused on the stripes Jesus bore and accept His beatings as payment in full for whatever I'm battling.

> Praying in tongues can release healing to your body. It releases strength to your soul and physical flesh.

When the spirit and soul are in alignment with God, the body has no vote. If your body is under attack, or you are injured or being physically challenged in any way, praying in tongues can help you enter into the deep, healing, recuperative rest of God. That rest unlocks the faith that connects you to the healing virtue of Jesus that is already resident in your inner man. Your gift of tongues is definitely a *power tool* for healing. This works particularly well for you personally but can also be used when praying for others. You can release a healing, inner rest to another by praying in tongues.

In any battle our eyes need to stay on the Master, not on the problem. When praying concerning illness, I rarely give place to the diagnosis in my prayers. If I mention it at all, I may reference it at the beginning of my prayer saying something like, 'Lord, I bring Darla and this diagnosis of ovarian cancer before You.' I then begin to pray in tongues asking the Holy Spirit to show me my part in prayer for Darla. I first need to know if I have an assignment from God concerning her and then need to know how to pray strategically. That's where using my **power tools** is invaluable. Praying in tongues defines my assignment and keeps me focused.

I have been in full-time ministry for several years and have invested many hours of concentrated study on what the Bible has to say about healing. Just from my natural knowledge of what the Bible teaches and from my past experiences concerning healing, I can pray several things from memory for someone battling an illness like ovarian cancer, but those kinds of prayers have sometimes proven to be wasted time and effort. I know that because I can see the fruit. Even though I can quote many Bible verses about healing, I have found that just randomly pulling out healing verses is somewhat like slinging a paintbrush full of paint against a barn hoping those hit-or-miss splatters will somehow paint the whole building.

Paul said, I therefore so run, not as uncertainly; so fight I, not as one that beateth the air. (1 Corinthians 9:26).

When I just start firing out healing scriptures, it can be somewhat like beating the air. My prayers sound more desperate than targeted. I have never been in faith and desperation at the same time. Although using Scripture is never wrong, strategically using the specific Word of God for a given situation is far more productive. It produces results. Just as our loving heavenly Father provided fresh manna for the Israelites every day in the wilderness, He has fresh manna for every situation we face.

I am going to give you a fictitious example of what following a leading from the Holy Spirit might look like when praying for someone ill. Again, this is not a formula; it's an example. Please use it only as a guideline.

Let's use the fictitious situation I just mentioned. Darla has been diagnosed with ovarian cancer and I have been asked to pray for her. Once that I have confirmed that the Holy Spirit is calling me to pray for Darla, I usually begin my prayers with thanksgiving that the answer is already given and praise the Lord for His everlasting goodness to release that answer to her. I might then ask the Father to bring wholeness to her body to glorify Jesus and to show me anything I need to see. *'He shall glorify me: for he shall receive of mine, and shall shew it unto you'* (John 16:14). After that, I wouldn't do anything else but pray in tongues and be still before Him. *'Be still and know that I am God: I will be exalted among the heathen, I will be exalted in the earth'* (Psalm 46:10). I would then wait for a leading or unction to know how to continue. As I pray, I yield my heart to the Holy Spirit, listening intently, and will repeat out loud in English anything I hear Him say. That may begin a dialogue something like this:

I might hear the Holy Spirit say a single word, 'release.' I would then perhaps pray, "Lord, I ask that You release the healing virtue of Jesus in Darla and glorify Him in her physical body." From there, I would pray in tongues again until I have another response from Him. I describe it as somewhat like playing tennis. I return to the Holy Spirit exactly what He gives me. He gave me the 'release' and I give the exact same word back to Him. If I don't correctly appropriate the word He gives me, He'll correct me. Don't be concerned about doing it wrong; I promise you, you will do it wrong many times, but if your heart is open, the Holy Spirit will always redirect you. Once I know that I'm speaking His Word correctly, He may then lead me to pray something like this:

1. That Darla be strengthened in her weakness (Romans 8:26)

2. She receive strength, healing, and hope (1 Corinthians 14:4; Luke 4:18; Romans 15:13)

3. Her faith be built to receive healing (Jude 20)

4. She not be overcome by the wiles of the enemy (Ephesians 6:11)

I will ask, pray in tongues, listen to what the Holy Spirit deposits in my heart, and follow Him, repeating out loud what He says. Speaking what He says is a powerful resource of the Spirit. Often, the Holy Spirit will lead my prayer in a direction I didn't perceive at all. That is more common than rare. The Holy Spirit knows everything about a situation, where I may know little or nothing at all. I have learned not to question or debate His leading. I just follow Him. If He says, 'It's green,' then it's green to me even if everything I see in the natural is yellow. I don't debate Him. I used to do that and learned some very hard lessons that way, so I encourage you to let Him lead. He really does know what He's doing. It's humbling to find out how much you don't know. Resist the urge to yield to your natural reasoning or resort to natural understanding; trust me, it is profoundly limited.

Once I yield myself to the Holy Spirit and follow His lead, He'll take over. All He's looking for is willing and compliant partners. As I choose to agree with the Holy Spirit, I become aware that He is working and I am right there with Him. Again, the process reminds me somewhat of two highly trained and experienced ballroom dancers. The movement is fluid and flawless. The Holy Spirit and I begin to be one voice declaring God's will into Darla's situation. I am not interjecting my own will or opinions into the mix. In my native tongue, I mostly repeat what I hear the Holy Spirit say and rarely add anything to it except words of thanksgiving. I just keep my heart and mind on the finished work of Calvary. That finished work knows what it is designed to do in Darla's body.

When I'm not hearing something specific, I might repeat a verse concerning what the Holy Spirit can do in the situation; perhaps something from the list in chapter 11, like asking the Father to give Darla hope. *'Now the God of hope fill you with all joy and peace in believing, that ye may abound in hope, through the power of the Holy Ghost'* (Romans 15:13).

Having the list from chapter 11 at ready access will prove very helpful to you. Remember, you are co-laboring with the Holy Spirit so knowing what He does in the earth is of utmost importance to you. If you hear an instruction that is contrary to what Scripture says about Him, you can discount it immediately. The list in chapter 11 is not comprehensive, and you'll soon be adding to it as you learn more about this sweet union and communion with the Holy Spirit, keeping in mind that everything you add will be confirmed by the written Word of God.

> Remember, you are co-laboring with the Holy Spirit so knowing what He does in the earth is of utmost importance to you.

I would expect the Holy Spirit to draw me to prayer as many times as necessary for Darla, and would not arbitrarily pray for her on my own. Some situations require numerous times of prayer, but the assignments are never arduous when I'm using my *power tools*. I can pray for Darla and function normally in my everyday routine. My heart stays connected to the answer, not the problem, and my co-laboring with the Holy Spirit seems somewhat like taking a walk with a dear friend.

Is It My Head or My Heart?

Co-laboring with the Holy Spirit is a work of the heart, not a work of the head. It takes practice to know the difference. You can pray in tongues and think natural thoughts at the same time, but your spirit man is not connected to your brain. The Holy Spirit is God. He is a Spirit and speaks to your spirit man, not to your brain. You need to learn how to identify the inner witness of the Holy Spirit speaking to your spirit man and learn how to follow His voice. I think one of the best ways to do that is to jump into the deep end of the pool. By that I mean, step out in faith and practice. Simply ask, be still, listen and do what you hear. Then check your fruit. Was your prayer productive? That's the best test I know.

One way I discern if I'm hearing from God or from my own soul is by identifying where in my natural physical body I am hearing that voice. Is the voice coming from my natural brain, or am I hearing it from someplace inside me? Concentrate on locating where the voice originates. Are you hearing from the core of your being? As I engage my spirit man with my tongues, I hear the Holy Spirit speak inside the center of my being; I hear in my heart. I rarely hear the Lord speak audibly. I have only heard Him speak to me audibly twice, and both times every cell in my body was at full attention and I heard Him clearly. I don't hear the Holy Spirit speak to me with my natural ears, I hear Him deep inside and I rarely hear several distinct words at a time. Instead, I receive a few words, or an impression, or a 'knowing.' I might see an image. Sometimes, something natural will come to my remembrance that awakens me to insight or knowledge. The Holy Spirit may remind me of another situation not at all related to the one in my heart at the time and I'll see something that is common between the two. There may be several 'tweaks' like that as I pray. I just yield my heart and follow His lead then do what He says to do, or say what He says to say.

The Holy Spirit sometimes speaks to me through nature. I often hear Him clearly while working in my yard or walking on the beach. He will speak to you in whatever gets your attention.

If you play a musical instrument, pray in tongues while playing, unless, of course, you play a wind instrument. You can't play a wind instrument and use your *power tools* at the same time.

Remember, if you're praying in genuine, Holy Spirit tongues, your physical tongue moves as you speak. God often communicates through music and I've had musicians tell me that God spoke to them clearly while they played and prayed in tongues. 'Play and Pray' is a great way for those who are musically gifted to connect with the Holy Spirit. Singers should sing in tongues and anticipate hearing the Holy Spirit speak in the notes they hear.

It has not been my experience, but I've had others tell me, that the Holy Spirit directs their prayers through colors or smells. Regardless of how the Holy Spirit begins His side of the dialogue, I simply choose to follow Him. It is a choice I must make. The process ends if I don't choose to follow Him. He never forces me, He just invites and I make a free will decision to redirect my heart to follow in the path He illuminates before me. I choose, then pray in tongues, and He leads me.

If I'm praying about an assignment from the Lord and am in a position to take notes, I do. Sometimes I don't have a pen and paper but might have my phone handy and will use a recorder application to record what the Holy Spirit says to me. This is a crucial part of the process for me. Most prayer assignments are more than a 'one-shot deal,' and prayer times for a specific situation may be days or even weeks apart. For that reason, reviewing what the Holy Spirit gave me earlier about the situation affords me the opportunity to pick right up with the last revelation He gave me and not have to go back and cover the same ground again. I'm definitely not a big fan of reinventing the wheel. His previous words then become a 'jumping off point' for where He will take me next.

I believe that recording what the Holy Spirit gives me shows Him honor, and it also demonstrates my commitment to work with Him. I am faithful to record what He gives me. In doing that, I don't have to depend upon my natural memory to bring me up to speed. The Holy Spirit is certainly more than able to bring all things to my remembrance, but I find He is pleased that I care enough about what He shows me to record it. Sometimes I'll be reading my notes from a previous prayer time and, before I finish, I have a complete answer to the need revealed to my heart without uttering another word of prayer. Those are really special times.

The real key to using your *power tools* effectively is hearing the Holy Spirit correctly and following Him precisely; just listen and do exactly what He says. It takes both time and training to hear the Holy Spirit accurately but, if you'll ask Him, your Divine Helper will meet you more than halfway. Your first major investment is to set aside all distractions and give Him time. Learning how to accurately co-labor with the Holy Spirit is not done on the fly but, once you develop a working relationship with Him, praying in this manner will become so natural it will almost seem to be second nature to you. As you mature in this, you will be able to pray and receive quickly. He's looking for co-laborers and He'll not make it difficult for you.

I am always humbled when God uses me in prayer for others. I have had more than a few occasions where He would thank me for being available. Let Him be able to say that about you. I've come to learn that the Holy Spirit isn't looking for the most talented or the most educated; He's looking for the ones who show up willing to work. Just tell the Holy Spirit that you're reporting for duty and you'll be amazed to find how quickly He'll come right alongside you and teach you how to co-labor with Him in our heavenly Father's vineyard. In a very short time, you'll be firing up your **power tools** and seeing the Kingdom of God come and His will done in *your* life.

FIRE UP YOUR POWER TOOLS

A STARTER PRAYER

I have mentioned several times that you should ask God for His divine assistance in learning how to use your *power tools*. If you have not already done that, and are interested in living a strong and vibrant life in Christ, I encourage you to pray this prayer in your heart while you pray silently in tongues. You may have never done anything like that before, but try. I promise you can easily do both.

Dear Heavenly Father,

I come to You in the name of Jesus, the Master of the Church, and thank You for sending Your Spirit to be my helper. I ask You to open my heart to the greatness of Your mighty power available to me in Him. Teach me how to work with the Holy Spirit and through Him cause me to be strengthened with might in my inner man that Christ may live in my heart in faith and that I might be rooted and grounded in love (Ephesians 3:16-17).

I desire to serve You well and I ask for clarity of heart to hear the Holy Spirit speak to me and show me Your will for my life. I don't want to be powerless in this life and I ask that You strengthen me with all might according to Your glorious power and teach me how to use my *power tools* to co-labor with the Holy Spirit.

I believe that you hear me and I receive my request by faith and thank You for it. Amen.

Enjoy the Ride!

I Find No Fault
The Liberating Power of Forgiveness

Linda Markowitz
with Ray Ciaramaglia

What would you do if you received the call no parent wants to receive; a call telling you that your child is dead?

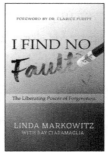

What would you do if the Lord asks you to do something totally unreasonable and impossible?

This book reveals one woman's answers to those questions and tells the story of an agonizing decision to trust God and the remarkable outcome of simply agreeing with Him.

Find both of Linda's books at **Amazon.com**

Made in the USA
Columbia, SC
14 June 2020

11098214R00078